# Entrepreneurs Creating Educational Innovation

Laura Hougaz

# Entrepreneurs Creating Educational Innovation

Case Studies From Australia

Laura Hougaz
Study Connections
Melbourne, VIC, Australia

ISBN 978-3-030-28653-8    ISBN 978-3-030-28655-2 (eBook)
https://doi.org/10.1007/978-3-030-28655-2

© Springer Nature Switzerland AG 2020

This work is subject to copyright. All rights are reserved by the Publisher, whether the whole or part of the material is concerned, specifically the rights of translation, reprinting, reuse of illustrations, recitation, broadcasting, reproduction on microfilms or in any other physical way, and transmission or information storage and retrieval, electronic adaptation, computer software, or by similar or dissimilar methodology now known or hereafter developed.

The use of general descriptive names, registered names, trademarks, service marks, etc. in this publication does not imply, even in the absence of a specific statement, that such names are exempt from the relevant protective laws and regulations and therefore free for general use.

The publisher, the authors, and the editors are safe to assume that the advice and information in this book are believed to be true and accurate at the date of publication. Neither the publisher nor the authors or the editors give a warranty, express or implied, with respect to the material contained herein or for any errors or omissions that may have been made. The publisher remains neutral with regard to jurisdictional claims in published maps and institutional affiliations.

This Springer imprint is published by the registered company Springer Nature Switzerland AG.
The registered company address is: Gewerbestrasse 11, 6330 Cham, Switzerland

# Preface

Entrepreneurs play a critical role in the economy. By identifying opportunities and exploiting them, they fulfil social and economic needs. In Australia, as in many other parts of the world, we are accustomed to private as well as government investment in primary and secondary education. However, little is generally known about venture capitalists and the investments that support the creation of a vigorous independent tertiary education sector and the role that entrepreneurs play in driving change in this sector.

In many countries, including Australia, higher education is being transformed, and over recent decades, universities have been gradually facing imminent disruption through new technologies and entrepreneurial activities.

> A long pedigree and fine stone buildings offer little defence against the restless inventiveness of entrepreneurs, who see opportunities to remake the higher education model conceived in Australia in 1850 (Davis, 2017, p. 93).

With the increasing demand worldwide to access quality education and training at both vocational and higher educational levels, coupled with the enlarged market-based competition and prioritising of qualifications and pathways, entrepreneurs with a particular interest in education have entered and expanded the market, diversifying and innovating tertiary education and training in Australia and internationally, capitalising on the increasing desire for individual security and prosperity. Their entrepreneurial accomplishments have contributed directly to the recent and substantial growth of the independent tertiary education sector in Australia and indirectly to the economic growth of the nation. How they identify, engage with, and capture opportunities in the field of tertiary education remains unexplored, their entrepreneurial achievements remain largely ignored, and the independent tertiary education sector which they have created and diversified, and to which they make an ongoing valuable contribution, remains fundamentally underestimated.

In this book I recognise the contribution that such entrepreneurs have made in diversifying and redefining the tertiary education landscape in Australia. I explore how and why entrepreneurs have entered a new environment which traditionally has been a public sector. I offer an understanding of the ways in which such entrepreneurs have explored, and engaged with opportunities that they have identified in tertiary education, and created new businesses that are also, at the same time, educational organisations. These entrepreneurs have not only created new businesses, but their economic actions are having a noticeable social and economic impact on the society, economy and educational profile of Australia.

This book offers insight into the distinctive ways in which entrepreneurs have identified new opportunities in the independent tertiary education and training sector and how their contribution is redefining the Australian tertiary education sector.

Part I of the book comprises an introductory chapter that provides a brief overview of the tertiary education sector in Australia, discussing the rapid growth of the independent sector and its contribution to the diversification of offerings for tertiary students.

Part II of the book comprises seven case studies of some of Australia's well-known independent tertiary institutions, presenting the entrepreneurs who have founded them and developed them into notable and reputable educational enterprises.

The case studies are based on in-depth interviews, supported by secondary data from books, websites, magazine and newspaper articles to capture the variety and richness of independent education entrepreneurship.

These case studies aim to broaden our understanding of the phenomenon of independent tertiary education in Australia and around the world and the role that entrepreneurs have played. The case studies will also make an important contribution to the topic of entrepreneurship.

Melbourne, VIC, Australia  Laura Hougaz
24 May 2019

## Reference

Davis, G. (2017). *The Australian idea of a university*. Carlton, VIC: Melbourne University Publishing.

# Acknowledgements

I am grateful to the inspirational entrepreneurs who have founded independent tertiary educational institutions around Australia who contributed to this book, in particular those who comprise the case studies, for their participation and support in sharing their personal and professional stories that underpin this work.

My sincere appreciation to Prof Kwong Lee Dow (University of Melbourne) for his encouragement and constructive comments. Thanks also to Dr Peter Ryan (Higher Education Leadership Institute—HELI) for his practical and helpful advice and to John-Paul Hougaz for his valuable assistance in editing the manuscript.

On a personal note, I dedicate this book to my loving and long-time friend and partner Louis and my two wonderful and supporting children, John-Paul and Maxine, who have shared their lives, over the last few years, with this book.

Finally, I thank my publishers, Springer International Publishing. I appreciate that they believed in me to provide the leadership and knowledge to make this book a reality.

# Contents

**Part I Overview**

**1 The Tertiary Education Landscape in Australia** .............. 3
   1.1 Introduction to Tertiary Education in Australia ............ 3
   1.2 The Expansion and Diversification of Tertiary Education in Australia ................................................. 6
      1.2.1 The Public Tertiary Education Sector ............... 6
      1.2.2 The Independent Tertiary Education Sector .......... 8
   1.3 Entrepreneurship in Tertiary Education .................... 12
   References ................................................. 14

**2 Entrepreneurs Create Educational Innovation** ............... 19
   2.1 Entrepreneurs Identify Opportunities in the Tertiary Education Sector ................................................. 19
   2.2 The Case Studies in This Book ........................... 26
   References ................................................. 28

**Part II Case Studies**

**3 Dr Martin Cass: JMC Academy** ........................... 31
   3.1 About JMC ........................................... 31
   3.2 The Entrepreneurial Journey Begins ...................... 32
   3.3 The Education Business Grows .......................... 33
   3.4 A Team Effort ........................................ 35
   3.5 JMC Grows .......................................... 38
   3.6 Martin Cass: The Entrepreneur .......................... 41
   Reference ................................................. 42

**4 Mathew Jacobson: Ducere Global Business School** ........... 43
   4.1 About Ducere Global Business School .................... 43
   4.2 The Ducere Foundation ................................ 44
   4.3 The Entrepreneurial Journey Begins ...................... 48
   4.4 From an Education Business to More than an Educational Enterprise ............................................. 50
   4.5 Mathew Jacobson: The Entrepreneur ..................... 52
   References ................................................. 54

| | | | |
|---|---|---|---|
| **5** | **Rod Jones: Navitas** | | 55 |
| | 5.1 About Navitas | | 55 |
| | 5.2 The Entrepreneurial Journey Begins | | 56 |
| | 5.3 Navitas Grows | | 60 |
| | 5.4 Rod Jones: The Entrepreneur | | 61 |
| | 5.5 Recognition for His Achievements | | 65 |
| | References | | 68 |
| **6** | **Julie Moss: Photography Studies College (Melbourne)** | | 69 |
| | 6.1 About Photography Studies College (Melbourne) | | 69 |
| | 6.2 The Entrepreneurial Journey Begins | | 70 |
| | 6.3 PSC Grows | | 74 |
| | 6.4 Julie Moss: The Entrepreneur | | 77 |
| | References | | 82 |
| **7** | **Sarina Russo: Sarina Russo Group** | | 83 |
| | 7.1 About the Sarina Russo Group of Companies | | 83 |
| | 7.2 The Entrepreneurial Journey Begins | | 84 |
| | 7.3 The Sarina Russo Group Grows | | 88 |
| | 7.4 Sarina Russo: The Entrepreneur | | 90 |
| | 7.5 Recognition for Her Achievements | | 92 |
| | References | | 95 |
| **8** | **Greg Quigley: Jazz Music Institute** | | 97 |
| | 8.1 About Jazz Music Institute (JMI) | | 97 |
| | 8.2 The Entrepreneurial Journey Begins | | 99 |
| | 8.3 JMI Grows | | 102 |
| | 8.4 Greg Quigley: The Entrepreneur | | 110 |
| | References | | 112 |
| **9** | **Leanne Whitehouse: Whitehouse Institute of Design, Australia** | | 113 |
| | 9.1 About Whitehouse Institute of Design | | 113 |
| | 9.2 The Entrepreneurial Journey Begins | | 115 |
| | 9.3 Whitehouse Institute Grows | | 119 |
| | 9.4 Leanne Whitehouse: The Entrepreneur | | 119 |
| | 9.5 Recognition of Her Achievements | | 121 |
| | References | | 124 |
| **10** | **Conclusion** | | 125 |
| | References | | 128 |

# About the Author

**Laura Hougaz** is an experienced senior academic, researcher and manager with extensive experience in the public and private Australian higher education sectors. She has received university and community awards including the Vice Chancellor's Prize for Excellence in Internationalisation, and has attracted and managed large research projects and study programs. Laura has published in a broad range of areas, from entrepreneurship to family business, and issues related to higher education.

# Part I
# Overview

# The Tertiary Education Landscape in Australia

## 1.1 Introduction to Tertiary Education in Australia

In an increasingly competitive global knowledge economy driven by 'the widening, deepening and speeding up of world wide interconnectedness' (Held, McGrew, Goldblatt, & Perraton, 1999, p. 2), new organisations, including those in the educational and training sector, are being formed and reshaped at a rapid rate, in response to evolving demands for knowledge-intensive production.

Defining *independent tertiary education* (often referred to as *private tertiary education*) is not an easy task (Altbach, 1999; Geiger, 1986; Levy, 1986b, 1999, 2002, 2013). One reason is that the term *tertiary education* in some countries only refers to the university (higher education) sector, while in other countries, it may include a college (USA), polytechnic (UK) or TAFE (Technical and Further Education—Australia) sector. A second reason is that the boundaries between tertiary institutions delivering public and independent tertiary education are gradually becoming more unclear and overlapping. A third reason is that tertiary education in countries across the world is the product of different histories and contexts; therefore, one universal definition is not applicable (Altbach, 1999).

Traditionally, public tertiary education institutions have been established by government legislation, owned and funded by government and registered as not-for-profit organisations. Independent tertiary institutions are, by and large, incorporated as a company, owned by private interests, funded by private or student fees and are for-profit organisations, with the ability to make distributions to owners or shareholders.

Recently, however, the boundaries between the two sectors are becoming increasingly more blurred, with an active and entrepreneurial independent sector moving into areas of education traditionally only offered by the public sector, with various degrees of government regulation over the independent sector (Altbach, 1999; Levy, 1986b, 2002, 2003, 2006, 2013).

Maldonado-Maldonado (2004) also point to the broad spectrum of organisational forms that exist across the tertiary sector. At one end are the public tertiary institutions—traditional, well-established universities predominantly funded by the government—and at the other end is the independent sector, often fully funded by private capital. In between is a wide array of public–private mixes with varying models and scale of operations, which obscure, and often confuse, the boundaries between public and independent sectors.

The blending of the two sectors (public and independent) is increasing, partly due to the gradual withdrawal of government funding from public providers, and partly as public providers develop dynamic collaborations with the independent sector, as well as their own private activities, courses and enterprises. Forms of privatisation by the public sector differ in scope and objective. These range from partnerships with private organisations, such as theology colleges offering courses accredited in public institutions, or with colleges that deliver courses preparing students (predominantly international) to *articulate* into public higher education, to the establishment of their own separate, independent companies that generate income by delivering a particular service or course of study, for example TESL (Teaching of English as a Second Language), Massive Online Open Courses (MOOCs) with unlimited participation and open access and micro-credential programs and digital badging which reflect competence in particular skills or knowledge and potentially pave personal new learning pathways into formal courses. These vibrant and productive innovations are blurring the public–independent divide by redesigning tertiary education.

The fundamental distinction, however, between public and independent tertiary education is related to funding, the difference being between non-profit education (private or public) and for-profit education. As Morey (2004) notes, 'for profit institutions provide education to make money, while traditional colleges and universities accept money to provide an education' (p. 143). Public institutions are non-profit: the government subsidises the overall costs borne by public institutions, such as tuition fees, research, infrastructure and student activities. They offer full-fee recovery courses and activities. Independent providers receive no government operating grants and generally fund all their own expenses to establish and operate their institutes, and students at independent institutions predominantly pay full tuition fees and associated costs (although subsidised National Priorities Pool—NPP—places are available at some independent institutions in Australia). The difference in funding determines decisions related to governance, curriculum offerings and delivery, student admissions and services, staffing and professional development and non-teaching activities. However, over the past decade, many governments have endorsed policies that support the cost sharing of tuition fees through student loans for tertiary education. Moreover, some independent institutions are also partly or fully sponsored by religious organisations, with some elite independent institutions often undertaking government-sponsored research (Altbach, 1999).

Generally, this funding distinction between public and private, which was once clear-cut, is nowadays not as evident. Most public higher education institutions now charge fees to their students and some independent institutions receive funds from governments (Levy, 1986a). In addition, some independent higher education institutions, such as in Holland and Belgium, receive funds from their governments, similar to the public counterparts (Geiger, 1986). In conclusion, funding as a sole criterion appears inadequate in determining the form of tertiary education institution.

The legal ownership and form of corporate structure of tertiary education institutions may be a less ambiguous criterion when classifying institutions as public or independent (Levy, 1986b). However, as governments gradually assumed responsibility for funding tertiary education, even the early collegial model of university governance led by scholars, typical of traditional universities such as Oxford and Cambridge in the UK, changed, gradually evolving towards a more modern and universal model, with the university as a public corporation. As universities come to grips with the need to be more efficient and competitive, councils are transforming into board of directors, comprising external business people who, together with senior management, are focusing more and more on profitability. As Thornton (2012) notes, the concept of higher education has also transformed over time: 'The market and competition policy have allowed the commercial-in-confidence norms of business to corrode the idea of education as a public good'.

As Altbach (1999) points out, across the world, in different countries there are variations in forms of ownership. Independent institutions may be owned by either non-profit or profit-making agencies or a combination of both. While being not-for-profit institutions, both the University of Buckingham (1983) in the UK and Bond University (1987) in Australia have been founded by private developers and funded largely with private fees. Their governance structures, however, are akin to public corporation models found in state-funded universities.

Independent higher education institutions founded as commercial enterprises are generally funded by commercial companies or investors. Here too, there are significant variations in functions, missions and character of institutions, which have profound implications for corporate governance. In the case of the University of Phoenix (1976), owned by the Apollo Group, its main goal is to make higher education more accessible to social groups that previously did not have opportunities to participate. Its social function is similar to that of universities; however, its educational and support functions are as a commercial enterprise, meeting targets and expecting regular financial returns.

In some parts of the world, such as in Latin America, the religiously affiliated not-for-profit independent colleges and universities, legally established and financially supported by religious organisations, are in large numbers. Originally driven by the need for religious based education, and later by the massification of tertiary education and decreasing state funding for students, the religious independent sector consolidated into 'the creation of a non-elite secular subsector based mainly on absorbing demand unmet in the public sector' (Levy, 1993, p. 15). In Australia, the Australian Catholic University (ACU) gained university status in 1991, having formed from an amalgamation of four Catholic tertiary institutions. It is now a publicly funded university that operates as a company limited by guarantee, a not-for-profit organisation that overlaps the public/private divide.

As is evident, the public tertiary sector is nominally public, but in practice has shifted to a public–private hybrid in response to pressures deriving from the progressive withdrawal of government funding for public institutions. Educational models and roles are steadily changing, with the public and independent sectors collaborating more closely in the development and delivery of teaching. Marginson (2007) recognises that 'regardless of formal ownership or fee systems, a substantial part of the goods produced in Higher Education are [both] private [and public] goods' (p. 322). According to Newman and Couturier (2001) in future, traditional universities and independent institutions will become more closely intertwined and largely indistinguishable.

In this evolving tertiary education landscape where the divide between public and independent is becoming increasingly blurred, the number of for-profit tertiary education institutions has been steadily growing.

## 1.2 The Expansion and Diversification of Tertiary Education in Australia

### 1.2.1 The Public Tertiary Education Sector

Tertiary education in most nations is understood as a 'public sector' (with the notable exception of the USA). In Australia, the public tertiary education sector comprises TAFEs and universities, funded predominantly by, reliant on and responsible to the Australian State governments (for vocational education) and the Federal government (for higher education).

According to a recent Australian survey (Australian Bureau of Statistics, 2017), it was estimated that, of the 14.5 million people aged 20–64 years in Australia, 9.6 million (two in three Australians or 66%) have attained at least one tertiary qualification. Of these, 62% have attained a Certificate III qualification or higher, and 31% have attained a bachelor's degree qualification or higher. The survey also showed that the number of women holding tertiary qualifications continued to grow at a much faster rate than that of men, with 35% of women and 28% of men having attained a bachelor's degree or higher.

Of the estimated 15.9 million people aged 15–64 years in Australia, over 3 million, or nearly 1 in 5 (19%), were enrolled in formal study. Nearly three-quarters (71%) were studying non-school qualifications: two in five people (40%) were enrolled in a university degree, and one in five people were enrolled in a vocational qualification (20%). Approximately 1.2 million (41%) were attending a higher education institution, 884,000 (29%) were at school, 474,400 (16%) were at TAFE institutions and 404,200 (13%) were at other educational institutions or organisations.

Survey results released in 2013 (Australian Bureau of Statistics, 2013) estimated that eight million people aged 15–74 years, or just under half of Australia's working age population, undertook some type of formal and informal study or training over 12 months. Of these, 3.7 million (22%) participated in formal learning, 4.6 million (27%) in work-related training and 1.4 million (8.4%) undertook personal interest learning. Participation in work-related training was the highest for those aged between 25 and 54 years, with around a third (33%) of this group having participated

## 1.2 The Expansion and Diversification of Tertiary Education in Australia

in work-related training. Participation in work-related training varied according to occupation, industry and size of business. In industry, for example, just over half of those working in education, public administration, mining and health care had undertaken training, and one in six people employed in the agriculture, forestry and fishing industry. The same survey also reveals that more women than men are engaged in personal interest learning, with the most common reasons being personal development (59%) and enjoyment or interest (37%).

In Australia, in the 1970s, only a few per cent of the adult population held a degree. Under the Hawke government (1983–1991), a series of structural changes driven by the then Education Minister John Dawkins aimed to change the VET sector to an 'open training market' in which TAFE would compete with independent registered training organisations (RTOs). During this time, tertiary tuition fees were reintroduced[1] (Goozee, 2001).

By 2011, more than a third of young adults had graduated with a degree.

> Young people from working class families are now much more likely to go to university than people from any background within living memory. At least in middle-class families the pressure to go to university has increased. There may be a loss of communal standing from not enrolling, rather than a gain from doing so. For those who continue their education, there are hierarchies of institutions and courses, with many students wanting to 'get the most out of likely year 12 result' (Norton & Cakitaki, 2016, p. 59).

Over the past 20 years, the ever shifting political and economic environment has led to greater movement and change in the tertiary education sector, with student numbers, both domestic and international, more than doubling.

Australia is a leading destination for international students, attracting higher numbers every year. International education is Australia's third largest export industry generating more than AU$22 billion of economic activity in Australia.

In 2017, there were more than half a million full-fee-paying international students studying in Australia, an increase of approximately 15% compared with the previous year (Department of Education and Training, August 2017). The higher education sector had the largest share of Australia's international students (48%), with students coming predominantly from China and India. The vocational sector accounted for 26% of international student enrolments and 17% in English Language Intensive Courses for Overseas Students (ELICOS) (21%).

In response to the increasing importance of tertiary qualifications for national and international students, and the gradual expansion of access and social equalisation of tertiary participation, a growing demand for tertiary education places within and outside the traditional public sector has been taking place. Recent research

---

[1] Tuition fees at university and technical colleges (pre-TAFEs) had been abolished in Australia by the Whitlam Labour Government in 1974. It also established the Commonwealth's full responsibility for university funding. In 1989, the Hawke Labour Government reintroduced the fees, and established the Higher Education Contributions Scheme (HECS), a new system to defer payment of student fees. This became known as the 'Dawkins Revolution'.

acknowledges the benefits, public and independent, of higher education (Norton, 2012; Norton & Cakitaki, 2016)—this is fast becoming a global trend.

### 1.2.2 The Independent Tertiary Education Sector

The intensifying massification and globalisation of tertiary education has led, in Australia as in numerous other countries, to a larger and diversified independent tertiary education system that can match the varied needs of business and individuals (Gupta, 2008; Hamdan, 2013; Khanna & Khemka, 2012; Kinser & Levy, 2005; Ryan, 2012; Triventi & Trivellato, 2012). Fundamentally this is due to the progressive withdrawal of funding from the public sector and the shift to demand-driven funding resulting from broad reforms in order to improve participation in tertiary education.

According to Geiger (1988), this growth is also driven by demand, which he identifies as: 'more', reflecting the unmet demand, in particular for higher education; 'different', in response to social, community and religious needs for diverse programs, flexible modes of delivery and accelerated routes to qualifications; and 'better', indicating attraction to innovative, targeted courses, linked to industry, with employment outcomes.

Davis (2017) acknowledges that the growth of the independent sector is in response to student demand for greater choice.

> Some students want vocationally orientated courses, more flexible delivery, access to faith-based qualifications rather than the liberal education promoted by public institutions. They look to private offerings (p. 82).

In Australia, over the past two decades, independent tertiary education has expanded at an accelerated pace, across both the vocational and higher education sectors. Currently, close to 10% of Australian higher education students are enrolled with independent providers—a percentage that has been growing steadily. The independent sector is also delivering practical and accessible education that responds to the needs of students. Recent student experience and graduate satisfaction survey results released by QILT (the Quality Indicators for Learning and Teaching) indicate that in the undergraduate space across all Australian universities and higher education providers, independent institutions lead, scoring 23 of the top 25 QILT rankings for overall quality, as well as 24 of the top 25 for student support.

Generally, public awareness of independent tertiary education providers has been steadily growing, nationally and internationally, as they become established as a significant and respected part of Australian higher education.

In 1987, in Australia there were six small independent institutions specialising in agriculture and teacher training (Marginson, 1997). Now, there are currently approximately 5000 registered training organisations (RTOs) delivering vocational education and training (VET) services (ASQA website, 2019); and 175 registered higher education institutions, comprising 55 self-accrediting institutions—including

## 1.2 The Expansion and Diversification of Tertiary Education in Australia

40 universities, two overseas universities, one specialist university and 12 non-university higher education providers; and 120 non-self-accrediting higher education institutions (TEQSA website, 2019), delivering across a range of jurisdictions, providing students with education and training that result in the full array of qualifications, from certificates and diplomas to bachelor's, master's and doctorate degrees that are recognised and accepted by industry and other educational institutions.

Independent RTOs are a quite diverse group, with significant variations in terms of the types of students they attract, the nature of the courses they offer, the funding sources that support this activity and the factors shaping their businesses. They consist of adult/community providers (includes adult education centres, adult migrant education providers, community access centres and community education providers), enterprise-based organisations (training centres within enterprises whose prime business focus is an industry other than education and training), industry organisations (includes industry associations, professional associations and group training companies), commercial training organisations (providers supplying fee-for-service programs to the general public) and other independent providers (including agricultural colleges, and providers associated with licensing authorities and local government). These offer a wide range of accredited and non-accredited VET courses. Most deliver in only one state/territory. In addition to their course offerings, many independent RTOs offer a wide range of student services. Training is largely delivered face-to-face, with some online delivery of teaching, mainly to part-time rather than full-time students. The majority of independent RTOs are small in terms of numbers of staff they employ, largely employing 20 or fewer staff.

'Independent Higher Education Providers' (IHEPs)—also referred to as 'Non-University Higher Education Providers' (NUHEPs)—comprising independent higher education 'universities', 'colleges' or 'institutes', as well as numerous publicly owned institutions, are also a very diverse group. More than half deliver vocational education and training in addition to higher education courses, approximately 60% offer postgraduate courses, almost two-thirds are registered with the Commonwealth Register of Institutions and Courses for Overseas Students (CRICOS) and approved to deliver courses to overseas students, 15% offer postgraduate research degrees and approximately 20% operate across multiple jurisdictions.

IHEPs tend to be specialised and offer choice and diversity by delivering sub-degree, degree and above qualifications around particular fields of study, industry and market segments, such as business and finance, legal studies, theology, natural therapies, counselling and psychotherapy, photography, jazz music, linguistics, energy resources, etc. rather than offering a full range of academic programs (Norton, 2012). Teaching is their major educational function, with courses underpinned by close industry links and a focus on employment outcomes for graduates.

Higher education can be a profitable business. A small number of educational providers are listed as companies on the Australian stock market: these include Navitas Limited, which owns 11 separate IHEPs delivering an extensive range of educational services; Seek Limited, offering flexible and online delivery of teaching programs in collaboration with universities; and Academies Australasia. Kaplan, which operates across Australia, is listed on the New York Stock Exchange as a wholly owned subsidiary of Graham Holdings Company (formerly the Washington Post Company), and Laureate Education (Laureate International Universities), one of the largest educational networks in the world spanning across 23 countries including Australia, is listed on the NASDAQ Stock Market.

Organisations such as Navitas offer *pathway* courses at diploma level in partnership with universities, preparing students for entry into the second year of a university course—students gain direct entry into the university and are awarded the equivalent first year of study. At the other end of the spectrum, other IHEPs offer solely postgraduate courses, for example the College of Law, which prepares graduates for legal practice.

Some highly esteemed, high-quality, multimillion-dollar independent education and training organisations are exemplars of Australia's existing and potential global leadership and innovation in independent tertiary education today. They range from large, publicly listed groups of training organisations to small, niche colleges. Some are large, multi-campus, well-known universities such as Bond University, Notre Dame University and the collegiate University of Divinity.[2] Others are colleges that are the private arm of public universities, such as Monash College and UTS: Insearch. There are, moreover, groups of institutions under a common ownership, such as Torrens University, part of Laureate International Universities (LIU), offering courses in design, business, hospitality, health and English language training (partnering with Think Education, including Billy Blue College of Design, CATC Design School, William Blue College of Hospitality Management, the Australasian College of Natural Therapies, the Jansen Newman Institute with courses in counselling and psychotherapy); Study Group, with campuses across Europe, North America, Canada and Australasia, delivering programs across Australia at the ANU College, Australian College of Physical Education (ACPE), Charles Sturt University Study Centres, University of Sydney Preparation Programs; and Navitas offering foundation studies programs, courses in health and community services, business and industry, counselling and psychotherapy, public safety, IT, creative media, etc. and partnerships with universities in Australia, the USA, the UK, Canada and New Zealand.

There is also a large variety of renowned institutions, some large, others small, some located on one campus, others multi campus, specialising in specific educational fields. Some deliver specialist awards, for example in theology and ministry, such as Avondale College, Australian College of Theology, Christian Heritage College, Adelaide College of Divinity, Alphacrucis College, and in liberal arts, for example Campion College Australia. Others deliver qualifications in exclusive fields, such as the Jazz Music Institute (JMI), Photography Studies College, Becker

---

[2]Founded as the Melbourne College of Divinity in 1910, it was awarded university status in 2012, becoming known as the University of Divinity.

Helicopters Pilot Academy, XLT Underwater Welding Training, Cairnmillar Institute (counselling, psychotherapy and trauma therapy), Whitehouse Institute of Design (fashion design, interior design and styling), JMC Academy (contemporary music and performance, audio engineering, game design, etc.), Marjorie Milner College (floristry, hairdressing and beauty), MEGT Institute (apprenticeships and traineeships in mechanical, plastering, electrical, energy and utilities), Charlton Brown (youth work, and child, aged and disability care) and Collarts—Australian College of Arts, Encompass College of Education and Training (disability care), amongst others. Their courses are varied, offering choice in areas of specialisation and modes of delivery.

Independent providers offer the full range of nationally accredited offerings: English Language Intensive Courses for Overseas Students (ELICOS), Pathways to university, a wide range of VET programs and higher education courses, foundation studies, primary or secondary school studies, awarding the full range of vocational qualifications (certificates and diplomas) and degrees (bachelor's, master's and doctorates).

Students studying at independent providers come from various backgrounds and are generally looking for a more personal experience: these include professionals looking to upskill to further their career opportunities, apprentices and school-leavers wanting to learn a trade, higher education students looking for an alternative to universities and international students seeking a more practical style of degree, with a set of job ready skills.

Independent providers have also played an important role in the provision of education to students of low socioeconomic status (SES) groups, with 12.5% of students at independent institutions from low SES backgrounds, compared to 15.1% of students at public institutions (Norton, 2010). This is a relatively high rate, given the level of assistance received by universities to cater for such groups.

It is important to note that the rise and accomplishments of the independent tertiary education sector have been achieved within an environment that has generally steered prospective students towards the public sector (universities and TAFEs).

Since 2012, in order to ensure consistency in quality across states and type of providers, both the public and independent tertiary education sectors are regulated nationally by the same regulatory agencies, TEQSA (Tertiary Education Quality and Standards Agency) for higher education and ASQA (Australian Skills Quality Authority) for vocational education and training.[3]

It is this highly blurred, very competitive and extremely regulated sector that entrepreneurs have entered over the past 20 years, identifying niche areas to explore, founding successful and innovative educational businesses that are 'more agile, more focused on student needs, and have a strong commercial or customer focused outlook' (Szekeres, 2012, p. 11).

---

[3]Some states still regulate their single jurisdiction RTOs, notably Victoria and Western Australia.

## 1.3 Entrepreneurship in Tertiary Education

According to Schumpeter, one of the twentieth century's great economic thinkers, an entrepreneur is a dynamic force that creates new combinations and produces additional value, thus fulfilling an economic function. Gartner (1989) states that the essential ingredient in entrepreneurship is that new organisations are created. Other researchers claim that the defining dimension of entrepreneurship is innovation (Kirzner, 1973), whereby the entrepreneur may identify an opportunity for profit rather than create one.

In seeking a definition for entrepreneurship, Sharma and Chrisman (1999) provide the following: '... acts of organizational creation, renewal or innovation that occur within or outside an existing organization' (p. 17), while Lyon, Lumpkin and Dess (2000, p. 1056) focus on the entrepreneurial orientation of a firm which comprises '... processes, structures and/or behaviours that can be described as aggressive, innovative, proactive, risk taking, or autonomy seeking'.

Gartner (1985) draws attention to the fact that there is 'a tendency to underestimate the influence of external factors and overestimate the influence of internal or personal factors when making judgements about the behavior of other individuals' (p. 70), which indicates that entrepreneurship needs to be understood in its social and economic context.

To date, research on entrepreneurship and entrepreneurs has largely focused on industry and commerce, including corporate organisations. More recently, research has focused on formal institutions that facilitate social entrepreneurship (Estrin, Mickiewicz, & Stephan, 2013).

Limited research, however, has taken place about entrepreneurship in public sector entities, and in the education sector in particular. Corporate entrepreneurship in historically, largely publicly funded universities has only recently begun to be recognised as an emerging phenomenon (Cargill, 2007; Clark, 1998; Davis, 2017; Gibb, Haskins, & Robertson, 2009; Mars & Rios-Aguilar, 2010).

What it means to be an entrepreneurial university is unclear, and how to promote entrepreneurial activity in such traditional institutions is not easy to achieve.

> The overall management of university systems remains vested in individual national governments ... funding regimes, levels of investment, and human resource policies, can have critical impacts on their outputs, and in particular on their capacity to innovate, introduce organisational change and act entrepreneurially (Shattock, 2005, p. 14).

> The current system of centralised resource allocation and controls over tuition fees encourages 'a one size fits all' system (West, 1998, p. 88).

Although Australian public universities receive the greater part of their funding from the Australian federal government, they are also in part commercial ventures, with some receiving more than 50% of their revenue from commercial ventures (Harman & Harman, 2004).

Marginson and Considine (2000) argue that there are academic and organisational downsides to public universities increasing their dependence on industry and

## 1.3 Entrepreneurship in Tertiary Education

commerce, including issues of academic standards, especially when universities are receiving substantial revenue for services, and may feel under pressure in relation to the educational outcomes. Williams (2003) supports this view, confirming 'that the emergence of enterprise as a powerful and possibly dominant force in universities inevitably raises fundamental questions about their nature and purpose' (Shattock, 2005, p. 17).

Marginson (2007) claims that under certain conditions, the public/private divide in higher education may provide conditions of possibility for each other. Overall there is resistance by academics to this change in the nature of academic work, who find the concept of treating education as a 'commodity' difficult to accept (Lee & Rhoads, 2004). Unresolved issues about commercialising academic intellectual property, potential complications with royalties or profit sharing in organisations and complex internal bureaucratic financial controls and reporting processes are all impediments to a more rapid development of an entrepreneurial culture in universities (Clark, 2004; Shattock, 2005). Universities are becoming more aware that tertiary education has become a more fiercely competitive environment for funds, industry links, grants and the best quality of national and international staff and students.

Entrepreneurship may also be perceived as a characteristic *in* universities, not *of* universities. Perlman, Gueths, and Weber (1988) coined the term *academic intrapreneurs,* giving recognition to academics who create links with industry and raise external funding for research or teaching programs from new sources, adding to a culture of innovation and value creation. In this state of 'grand generalisations full of remote fogginess' and 'the gritty messy details of each university's complex reality' (Clark, 2003, p. 101), Clark has made an attempt to offer a model for practical guidance to university leaders on how to implement a culture of entrepreneurship in universities, suggesting that it is very important to 'balance interests across multiple levels' (Clark, 2004, p. 359).

Entrepreneurship in the VET sector is still largely unresearched, albeit numerous calls from governments, industry associations, business leaders as well as VET clients' senior managers are being made for VET organisations and individuals to be more innovative and entrepreneurial (Mitchell, 2007).

The above research literature provides an outline of entrepreneurship frameworks for thinking and discussing entrepreneurial behaviour in the public tertiary (predominantly university) sector. Interestingly, no literature has been identified on entrepreneurs/entrepreneurship in the independent tertiary education sector, covering both higher education and vocational education and training, perhaps due to the fact that it is a relatively recent phenomenon.

This book aims to provide some insights on entrepreneurs in independent tertiary education in Australia and thus fill an identified research gap.

This book focuses explicitly on the way entrepreneurs identify and exploit opportunities in the context of tertiary education and how they engage with the process of recombining opportunities to create and develop new educational frameworks (Schumpeter, 1934; Shane, 2003). It investigates how such contextual factors may promote, or inhibit, entrepreneurial thinking and actions in developing opportunities in tertiary education (Zhou, 2008).

Entrepreneurship is generally defined as identifying and exploiting opportunities which can be implemented through the entrepreneurial process, spanning from identifying opportunities to achieving venture growth (Baron, 2007; Shane, 2003).

Researchers offer two different perspectives on opportunity: some assert that entrepreneurs differ from others in their ability to perceive, or spot, opportunities that already exist in the system; others claim that they create the conditions that enable opportunities to arise, from nothing (Alvarez & Barney, 2007). Whether opportunities are created or simply identified is still widely debated (Read, Dew, Sarasvathy, & Wiltbank, 2009). Overall, however, our understanding of how new ideas emerge and how new opportunities get brought forward into commercialisable opportunities is limited (Shane & Venkataraman, 2000).

As Shane (2003) affirms:

> ... we could use more research that examines the actual decision to exploit opportunities rather than the static state of being an entrepreneur. (...) Research on the actual decision to exploit opportunities among people at risk of such exploitation would overcome many of the limitations inherent in much of our existing research on this topic, as well as provide more precise explanations for how individual differences influence the entrepreneurial process (p. 264).

Fundamentally research in entrepreneurship continues to focus on three basic questions: why some people, and not others, become entrepreneurs; why some people are able to recognise opportunities and decide to act to exploit them; and why some entrepreneurs become more successful than others (Baron, 2004).

It is generally agreed that entrepreneurs identify new opportunities and create new enterprises that contribute to economic development (Low & MacMillan, 1988; Shapiro, 2014). More recently, entrepreneurship is being regarded as a widespread driver of social change (Weber, Heinz, & DeSoucey, 2008).

This book addresses issues related to entrepreneurial behaviour in independent tertiary education and how entrepreneurs have recognised and explored potential business ideas in this sector and contributed to the disruption of tertiary education in Australia and internationally.

The book adds value to research and theory of entrepreneurship by filling a gap yet unresearched. It also gives well-earned recognition to entrepreneurial individuals who have made a valuable contribution to redefining the tertiary education sector.

## References

Altbach, P. G. (Ed.). (1999). *Private Prometheus: Private higher education and development in the 21st century*. No. 77. London: Greenwood Publishing Group.

Alvarez, S., & Barney, J. (2007). Discovery and creation: Alternative theories of entrepreneurial action. *Strategic Entrepreneurship Journal, 1*, 11–26.

Australian Bureau of Statistics (ABS). (2013, April). *Work-related training and adult learning, Australia*. Accessed February 2016, from http://www.abs.gov.au/ausstats/abs@.nsf/

# References

Latestproducts/4234.0Main%20Features1Apr%202013?opendocument& tabname=Summary&prodno=4234.0&issue=Apr%202013&num=&view=

Australian Bureau of Statistics (ABS). (2017). Accessed May 17, 2018, from https://www.abs.gov.au/

Australian Skills Quality Authority (ASQA). (2019). Accessed March 9, 2019, from https://www.asqa.gov.au/

Baron, R. A. (2004). Potential benefits of the cognitive perspective: Expanding entrepreneurship's array of conceptual tools. *Journal of Business Venturing, 19*, 169–172.

Baron, R. A. (2007). Entrepreneurship: A process perspective. In J. R. Baum, M. Frese, & R. A. Baron (Eds.), *The psychology of entrepreneurship* (pp. 19–39). Mahwah, NJ: Lawrence Erlbaum.

Cargill, B. J. (2007). *Models of organizational and managerial capability for the entrepreneurial university in Australia*. PhD Thesis, Swinburne University.

Clark, B. R. (1998). *Creating entrepreneurial universities: Organizational pathways of transformation*. Oxford: IAU Press and Pergamon.

Clark, B. R. (2003). Sustaining change in universities: Continuities in case studies and concepts. *Tertiary Education and Management, 9*(2), 99–116.

Clark, B. R. (2004). Delineating the character of the entrepreneurial university. *Higher Education Policy, 17*, 355–370.

Davis, G. (2017). *The Australian idea of a university*. Carlton, VIC: Melbourne University.

Estrin, S., Mickiewicz, T., & Stephan, U. (2013). Entrepreneurship, social capital, and institutions: Social and commercial entrepreneurship across nations. *Entrepreneurship Theory and Practice, 37*, 479–504.

Gartner, W. B. (1985). A conceptual framework for describing the phenomenon of new venture creation. *Academy of Management Review, 10*(4), 696–706.

Gartner, W. B. (1989). Some suggestions for research on entrepreneurial traits and characteristics. *Entrepreneurship Theory and Practice, 14*(1), 27–38.

Geiger, R. L. (1986). *Private sectors in higher education: Structure, function, and change in eight countries*. Ann Arbor: University of Michigan Press.

Geiger, R. L. (1988). Public and private sectors in higher education: A comparison of international patterns. *Higher Education, 17*, 699–711.

Gibb, A., Haskins, G., & Robertson, I. (2009). *Leading the entrepreneurial university*. Oxford: University of Oxford.

Goozee, G. (2001). *The development of TAFE in Australia*. Leabrook: National Centre for Vocational Education Research.

Gupta, A. (2008). International trends and private higher education in India. *International Journal for Education Management, 22*(6), 565–594.

Hamdan, A. (2013). An exploration into 'private' higher education in Saudi Arabia: Improving quality and accessibility? *The ACPET Journal for Private Higher Education, 2*(2), 33–44.

Harman, G., & Harman, K. (2004). Governments and universities as the main drivers of enhanced Australian university research commercialisation capability. *Journal of Higher Education Policy and Management, 26*(2), 153–169.

Held, D., McGrew, A., Goldblatt, D., & Perraton, J. (1999). *Global transformations: Politics, economics and culture*. Stanford: Stanford University Press.

Khanna, P., & Khemka, K. (2012). Enroll the world in for-profit universities. *Harvard Business Review, 90*(1–2), 62–62.

Kinser, K., & Levy, D. C. (2005). *The for-profit sector: US patterns and international echoes in higher education*. PROPHE Working Paper Series, 5. Program for Research on Private Higher Education.

Kirzner, I. M. (1973). *Competition and entrepreneurship*. Chicago, IL: University of Chicago.

Lee, J. L., & Rhoads, R. A. (2004). Faculty entrepreneurialism and the challenge to undergraduate education at research universities. *Research in Higher Education, 45*(7), 739–760.

Levy, D. C. (1986a). *Higher education and the state in Latin America: Private challenges to public dominance*. Chicago: University of Chicago Press.

Levy, D. C. (Ed.). (1986b). *Private education: Studies in choice and public policy*. New York: Oxford University Press.

Levy, D. C. (1993). Recent trends in the privatization of Latin American higher education: Solidification, breadth, and vigour. *Higher Education Policy, 6*(4), 12–19.

Levy, D. C. (1999). When private higher education does not bring organizational diversity. *Contributions to the Study of Education, 77*, 15–44.

Levy, D. C. (2002). *Unanticipated development: Perspectives on private higher education's emerging roles*. Program for Research on Private Higher Education (PROPHE) Working Paper, (1).

Levy, D. C. (2003). *Private higher education*. Encyclopedia of International Higher Education Systems and Institutions.

Levy, D. C. (2006). The unanticipated explosion: Private higher education's global surge. *Comparative Education Review, 50*(2), 217–240.

Levy, D. C. (2013). The decline of private higher education. *Higher Education Policy, 26*(1), 49–42.

Low, M. B., & MacMillan, I. C. (1988). Entrepreneurship: Past research and future challenges. *Journal of Management, 14*(2), 139–161.

Lyon, D. W., Lumpkin, G. T., & Dess, G. G. (2000). Enhancing entrepreneurial orientation research: Operationalizing and measuring a key strategic decision making process. *Journal of Management, 26*, 1055–1085.

Maldonado-Maldonado, A. (2004). *The influence of international organizations in the field of higher education in Latin America: The analysis of one epistemic community in Mexico*. Doctoral dissertation, Boston College.

Marginson, S. (1997). *Markets in education*. Sydney: Allen and Unwin.

Marginson, S. (2007). The public/private divide in higher education: A global revision. *Higher Education, 53*(3), 307–333.

Marginson, S., & Considine, M. (2000). *The enterprise university—Power, governance and reinvention in Australia*. Cambridge: Cambridge University Press.

Mars, M. M., & Rios-Aguilar, C. (2010). Academic entrepreneurship (re) defined: Significance and implications for the scholarship of higher education. *Higher Education, 59*(4), 441–460.

Mitchell, J. (2007). *Innovation and entrepreneurship in VET: A professional development guide for the Australian vocational education and training sector*. Adelaide: John Mitchell and Associates.

Morey, A. I. (2004). Globalization and the emergence of for-profit higher education. *Higher Education, 48*(1), 131–150.

Newman, F., & Couturier, L. K. (2001). The new competitive arena market forces invade the academy. *Change: The Magazine of Higher Learning, 33*(5), 10–17.

Norton, A. (2010). *Fair choices: A higher education funding system based on consistent principles*. ACPET Annual Conference, 2010.

Norton, A. (2012). *Graduate winners: Assessing the public and private benefits of higher education*. Melbourne: Grattan Institute.

Norton, A., & Cakitaki, B. (2016). *Mapping Australian higher education 2016*. Melbourne: Grattan Institute.

Perlman, B., Gueths, J., & Weber, D. A. (1988). *The academic intrapreneur: Strategy, innovation, and management in higher education*. New York: Praeger.

Read, S., Dew, N., Sarasvathy, S. D., & Wiltbank, R. (2009). Marketing under uncertainty: The logic of an effectual approach. *Journal of Marketing, 73*, 1–18.

Ryan, P. (2012). Growth and consolidation of the Australian private higher education sector. *The ACPET Journal for Private Higher Education, 1*(1), 5–11.

Schumpeter, J. A. (1934). *The theory of economic development* (R. Opie, Trans.). Cambridge, MA: Harvard University Press.

# References

Shane, S. (2003). *A general theory of entrepreneurship: The individual-opportunity nexus*. Northampton, MA: Edward Elgar.

Shane, S., & Venkataraman, S. (2000). The promise of entrepreneurship as a field of study. *Academy of Management Review, 25*(1), 217–226.

Shapiro, A. F. (2014). Self-employment and business cycle persistence: Does the composition of employment matter for economic recoveries? *Journal of Economic Dynamics and Control, 46*, 200–218.

Sharma, P., & Chrisman, J. J. (1999). Toward a reconciliation of the definitional issues in the field of corporate entrepreneurship. *Entrepreneurship Theory and Practice, 23*(3), 11–28.

Shattock, M. (2005). European universities for entrepreneurship: Their role in the Europe of knowledge the theoretical context. *Higher Education Management and Policy, 17*(3), 65–90.

Szekeres, J. (2012). *From public to private—The shifting sands of higher education*. Association for Tertiary Education Management and Tertiary Education Facilities Managers' Association, pp. 172–186.

Tertiary Education Quality and Standards Agency (TEQSA). (2019). Accessed January 9, 2019, from http://www.teqsa.gov.au/national-register

Thornton, M. (2012, March 28). Corporate hue colours issues of accountability. *The Australian, Higher Education Supplement*.

Triventi, M., & Trivellato, P. (2012). Does graduating from a private university make a difference? Evidence from Italy. *European Journal of Education, 47*(2), 260–276.

Weber, K., Heinz, K. L., & DeSoucey, M. (2008). Forage for thought: Mobilizing codes in the movement for grass-fed meat and dairy products. *Administrative Science Quarterly, 53*(3), 529–567.

West, R. (1998). *Learning for life: Review of higher education financing and policy: Final report*. Canberra: Department of Employment, Education, Training and Youth Affairs (DEETYA).

Williams, J. J. (2003). The higher education market in the United Kingdom. In P. Teixeira, B. Jongloed, D. Dill, & A. Amaral. *Markets in higher education: Rhetoric or reality?* Higher Education Dynamics. Dordrecht: Kluwer Academic.

Zhou, J. (2008). New look at creativity in the entrepreneurial process. *Strategic Entrepreneurship Journal, 2*(1), 1–5.

# Entrepreneurs Create Educational Innovation

## 2.1 Entrepreneurs Identify Opportunities in the Tertiary Education Sector

This chapter introduces the main topic of this book, which is *how* a number of entrepreneurs have identified and exploited opportunities in the tertiary education environment in Australia. Some of the comments also shed light on *why* they took the decision to enter a sector which has been, until the last 20 years, predominantly a publicly funded sector.

Through the numerous interviews conducted for this book, the entrepreneurs reveal a range of ways in which opportunities were identified, but in most cases, they dwell on the fact that opportunities 'came to them', rather than being purposely sought out. They reveal some driving forces that spurred them on to be open to, or search for alternatives or novelty.

Identifying an opportunity is 'essentially a creative process' (Hills, Shrader, & Lumpkin, 1999, p. 224) which is recognised as one of the pivotal elements of entrepreneurship (Kirzner, 1979; Shane, 2003) and is positively related to new firm formation (Lee, Florida, & Acs, 2004). An important condition for entrepreneurship is that once the opportunity is identified, it 'requires a decision by a person to act upon an opportunity because opportunities themselves lack agency' (Shane, 2003, p. 7). The exploitation of opportunities is regarded as the 'essence of entrepreneurship' (Shane & Venkataraman, 2000).

Opportunities may be *perceived* and *explored*, but are *exploited* only when a person decides to act. Accordingly, to frame the particular discussion in this book related to the identification of opportunities in the tertiary education sector, it is important to note that innovation primarily depends on the behaviour of the entrepreneur to *identify* and *act upon* opportunities.

It is widely acknowledged that acting on perceived opportunities is dependent on a range of individual differences, such as risk propensity, control beliefs or personality traits (Zhao & Seibert, 2006). Entrepreneurs are driven by a broad range of motives and career reasons (Carter, Gartner, Shaver, & Gatewood, 2003; Douglas &

Shepherd, 2002) in terms of their willingness to invest time, energy and money to start, and grow, a business (Zanakis, Renko, & Bullough, 2012). Hirschi and Fischer (2013) affirm there is considerable diversity in the relation between personal characteristics and entrepreneurial intentions and outcomes.

Some of the entrepreneurs in this book were motivated by a desire for independence.

> I had four jobs on the go—I was a legal secretary, a night school typing teacher, the body corporate secretary of my apartment block, and a cleaner of display units. I had no savings and was living from one pay packet to the next to finance the mortgage. Then I was fired from my legal secretary day job and my typing teaching job at night. [...]. I was determined and passionate about being financially independent. I started with a tremendous desire to never work as a secretary again. When I opened the school, I told myself, 'I'm going to give myself six months and if it doesn't work, I can always go back to a legal job'. But after six weeks, I knew it was going to work (Sarina Russo, Sarina Russo Group).

Others were driven by passion, an inner need to fulfil their dreams for what they really wanted to do or accomplish in life, other than what they were already doing, or where their life direction was taking them.

> As a teenager I developed a great passion for jazz, and I wanted to play. I used to go to jazz clubs, and then I bought a trumpet. And then began my whole journey. I went to a trumpet teacher, and what I wanted to learn was not what he could teach me. But I kept learning to play the trumpet and kept playing, and had this passion that what I really wanted to do was play jazz ... For years I was searching, asking 'how do you learn it?' I wanted to know the basics of how to play jazz (Greg Quigley, Jazz Music Institute).

Elizabeth Hoffman (*Australian College of Applied Animal Studies*) has always had a passion for horses and was always active in the industry. With a background in education, she saw opportunities to promote her interest amongst young people still at school.

> Horses are my passion, always have been ... Until a few years ago I was riding at international level, and I am also accredited as a level 2 coach. Students were coming in as riding students, and when they got to year 10 or 11 (final two years of secondary school), they had to make a decision whether they would continue riding, or they were going to do their VCE. I decided that we just had to introduce subjects in school. So we had the subject approved as a VCE subject (last year of secondary school).

As a university lecturer in equine management, she found out that the university had decided to close down the course. Fortunately a gap in the independent educational system opened up.

> I was lucky I had some good friends who were in the process of opening this place as a vet clinic . . . . It took me two years, I brought everything educational to this place. [...]. I had a passion for horses, and I am passionate educationalist. I've always done something a bit different, like introducing equine studies in schools, it was something that no one else had done . . . . It's like running a marathon, or climbing a mountain, it's there, so you climb it. The opportunity was there, so I did it.

## 2.1 Entrepreneurs Identify Opportunities in the Tertiary Education Sector

**Fig. 2.1** Author, Dr Laura Hougaz with Clive Langley, Managing Director, XLT Industrial Training, Perth, Western Australia (Photo courtesy of Clive Langley)

Others were driven by a perceived need to improve and fill a gap in the existing tertiary education system.

Clive Langley (*XLT Industrial Training*) initially identified an opening in skills training in the welding sector, specifically in how education interacted with industry (Fig. 2.1).

> I was driven by the serious shortage of skills in the workplace. The lack of training and skill in the workplace was immensely affecting efficiency. Most of the companies I would go to visit, I guarantee that I could increase the efficiency of their manpower and quality by 30% in 10 minutes just by talking to the person, and by just explaining what he was doing on the machine that he was using . . . . I had people wanting me to train them, in the workplace. So it came to a point that I thought 'I can have a business. I can make my mark here' . . .

Mathew Jacobson (*Ducere Global Business School*), qualified in law, established his entrepreneurial activity by identifying a niche area in online training. Along his entrepreneurial journey, one venture led to another.

> I started working in the e-learning space. I started a number of companies in online education. Utilizing my law background, we started to offer compliance training online.

E-learning is perfect for that .... [...] That evolved into getting into financial services training, which is a very regulated industry, so I built a private training organisation, Origin Human Resources, that focused on financial services training, but with accredited training, moving more into formal certification, and we worked all across Australia, a very large organisation, thousands of students a year. We were training many of the biggest companies, like PriceWaterhouseCoopers, KPMG, Goldman Sachs, auto finance companies, many of the big organisations were clients of ours. We had a premier product. ... I did that for six years, then sold it to a global public company (Talent2) in 2010. And then I thought 'What am I going to do?'. I wanted to do something not just for the purpose of working, but also for something that I was more interested in and passionate about. I have always been interested in working with at-risk kids, keeping them in school, I am big believer in not giving people a handout for charity, and that giving people food coupons for the rest of their life is not a good solution. A much better solution is giving people an education, a career path, and enable them to stand on their own feet. So the best concept of charity is to remove the need for charity. That was something that I was always very passionate about, and a strong philosophy for me. So I set up a new company, Ducere, with a focus purely on education, but with two very distinct sides to education. One is academic education, and that's effectively a business, that offers formal qualifications, fee-based. Through that academic business, we fully fund the Ducere Foundation that works to improve the quality of public education systems across African countries, a charity that we fund entirely. It's a self-sustainable, self-funded philanthropy .... [...] At Ducere we do online programs focused on business, management, leadership, entrepreneurship. We have documentary quality production, very high quality, very engaging. The critical aspect of our programs is the content itself, what you are learning, and who you are learning from. There is a role for academic learning, the theory and the underpinning knowledge, but that is a part of the whole puzzle, not the solution to learning. We believe that the best solution is a combination of both. Every lesson for us is taught by a world leader. Every single lesson, every element of every unit is taught by a president, a prime minister, a self-made billionaire, a marketing expert. We have people like Nobel prize winners, Harvard professors, people like Lindsay Fox, John Howard, incredible people from all over the world, Africa, Israel, Asia, America, Europe. ... That has never happened before, where you have an entire faculty that is made up of world leaders, and that is the differentiator between Ducere and what we see is happening out there in the market. We don't compete with universities, we don't think that universities are obsolete, or have to totally and radically redefine what it is they are doing. We believe that our program is a combination of the on campus experience, the academic underpinning, and also the real world experience. So we partner with higher education institutions, we don't compete with them.

Elaine Robb (*Encompass Community Services*) perceived the need to provide better options in the community services sector, in particular for the disadvantaged.

There was a clear need. It's very difficult when people come to you looking for assistance and support, with lots of ideas and ambition, and the options aren't available to them. I am a very impatient person at times. I don't like to sit around and wait, and I don't like to make promises I can't keep. So we decided to become a training organisation because the training being offered to people with disabilities was not really leading to anything for them. Lots of certificates of participation, but no real qualifications. That, combined with the training being provided to my staff, was not of a very high standard. I wanted to change that. We maintain at Encompass, that everything we do is quality. So we decided to become a registered training organisation.

## 2.1 Entrepreneurs Identify Opportunities in the Tertiary Education Sector

Greg Milner (*Marjorie Milner College*) comes from a family with a long tradition in flower growing and retailing. Greg and his family are committed to constantly innovate their educational business in such a competitive environment and strongly believe that new opportunities are perceived through their close links with the floristry industry. Greg and his family are recognised as industry leaders.

> The industry has always been, and I trust always will be, our strength . . . . When workplace training was introduced, we travelled across the state (of Victoria, now also Tasmania). I was enjoying that immensely because I was learning more, and it was opening up new doorways, and that was fantastic. We visited all the shops, so I knew all the employers. We kept visiting, and we still do today. It's important that you have a presence within your industry rather than stay in your office. You have to get out there, and they respect that . . . . [. . .] We're excited by the fact that we can teach students to be more innovative, but also to be competitive within an ever changing world. If you're not on your toes, you can be left behind in our area very quickly, and as a trainer, you can't afford to be. So we have to keep educating ourselves, and that is part of your innovation.

For Dianne Payne (*My Other Mum—MOM—Training College*), the opportunity presented itself as a reaction to a perceived professional need.

> I was providing child care. Then the Queensland government decided to change the way independent care was done. So I decided to become a training provider so that the family day care mums that were working with me on an independent basis could get qualified . . . . While I used to run the child care, I used to also run the Christmas Hospital Appeal. I wanted to continue my community service, and give something back to the community, and do my volunteer work. So I thought I would put out my initiative to the schools . . . and from there it just grew and grew and grew to where we are today. Basically, it was my community service, wanting to make a difference, and give parents choices in their child care requirements.

With her background experience as a TAFE lecturer in fashion design, Leanne Whitehouse (*Whitehouse Institute of Design*) was highly committed to developing better options for fashions design students. After travelling the world with a young baby and very little money saved up, she realised that working in a TAFE would not pay the rent. Her personal needs persuaded her to start her own educational business.

> My colleagues from TAFE and I had all discussed starting a private design school, and we knew that there was a great need for it. Once I had my baby, I realised that children are very expensive, and TAFE was not going to pay the rent, so I thought 'Well, I've talked about it for a long time, I certainly know a lot about teaching, and teaching design, and now is the time to go and do it'. [. . .] So I put one ad in Cleo (women's fashion magazine) and I had 25 phone calls, and 24 people gave me their money. I had not rented any premises. I knew nothing about business, absolutely nothing. I didn't have any furniture, so I went to an auction and bought all the furniture for the school . . . . That was in 1988 . . . . It took seven years of work for seven days a week for me, and I would never consider taking a day off . . . . We went from being one little room in Liverpool Street in the city (of Sydney), to taking over most of the building, and having outgrown that building, we moved to our beautiful premises in Surrey Hills.

Mel Koumides' previous experience in large multinational companies, managing the Asia Pacific region, was fundamental for the establishment of *Academia 21*. His late brother Philip had been the PEO for another private education organisation. Together they had the abilities and energy, confident that tertiary education could be delivered better.

> It wasn't an overnight thing. With my conservative approach, we were sitting down looking at the market, looking at what was happening, talking to Philip over many dinners. We felt it could be run better.... We wanted to focus on something that provided tangible skills and gave new opportunities to students. We weren't interested in just delivering a qualification. We were really interested in job outcomes, and we believed that if we focused on student care, everything else would fall in place.... It was also a time of choice for me: either go off on my own and build something, or focus and continue the employee, middle management-senior management path. But we saw the opportunity. Philip with his knowledge and background, that was a bit of a head start, and I sat down and crunched the numbers, over and over again, and did the risk analyses. The market was trending up, and we thought we could do it well.

Martin Cass (*JMC Academy*) acknowledges that for him, it was not a planned event, but rather a natural progression of events flowing one into the other, which led him, with an open mind, down the entrepreneurial path.

> I had a lot of experience in music from a very young age. My background is in audio engineering specifically in music production, producing live sound for touring acts, and ultimately taking bands into recording studios. I found a particular studio in Elizabeth Street, Surrey Hills in Sydney, that just happened to have the right gear and charge a reasonable rate. However, I realised that in this particular facility I never ever saw any other clients there. So I asked the owner why that was the case, and he said 'Well Martin, it's because I am going overseas, so I am not bringing in any other business, and in fact the business is for sale'. So, being young, and reasonably smart, I took some time to think about it, and ... in about 30 seconds I said 'I'll buy it!' .... I went away, and decided that the only way I could buy this place was to sell everything I owned ... I was young, and full of enthusiasm and arrogance and ego, why would I be scared? I didn't know what that meant.... On the very first night (of living on the premises), there was a knock on the door ... I opened the front door to find four young guys there, about 16 years old, saying: 'We are here for a class, and who are you?'. I asked them the same question, and they said: 'We have been paying the previous owner for one to one classes in how to produce audio' ... So I sat with them and looked through the notes, loosely called the curriculum, and it was just so obvious to me that it was back-to-front, all in the wrong order. So I took those notes, and we burnt them ... And that's how it began, an accident, a giant, but happy accident. There was no conscious decision to start a school, it just happened.

Rod Jones (*Navitas*) had worked in senior administrative positions in universities, in government and in independent education institutions. Through this varied background, he gained a thorough understanding of the education industry in Australia and began to notice gaps in the international education services industry.

> International students were pouring into Australia, and many were failing. It had nothing to do with academic ability, it was all the transitional issues they faced around language, culture, educational system, a completely different environment. They just didn't cope. High failure rates, clearly not in the interest of the students, nor of the institutions .... So I came up with a concept, which is what Navitas has built itself on, which involved taking the first year of the university degree, and delivering to the international students in a way that met

## 2.1 Entrepreneurs Identify Opportunities in the Tertiary Education Sector

their needs and requirements, by offering small classes, extra teaching hours, back-up English language support, a three semester calendar year. Effectively it was a winner from day one.

As Australian universities were not geared to deal with these issues, Rod recognised an opportunity for a company like Navitas.

> Getting universities to sign up to this concept, again, in part it was timing, but secondly, I had built a reputation as someone who knew what he was doing, and made things happen ... They recognised that there was an issue there that had to be dealt with ... Universities aren't geared up for this sort of thing, they are geared up to deal with the masses, and on top of that you have academics, and the last thing the academics want is a classroom full of people who are not coping. The whingeing and the complaining was another part of why the universities were saying 'if we can find a better way, firstly in reducing the failure rate, secondly, in assisting these students to get where they want to be, and thirdly, in taking away some of the issues that were confronting the academics who were not happy about what was happening', then it was going to be a winner. They basically said 'We'll give it a go!'.

Ryan Trainor (previously *Franklyn Scholar*, now *BSchool*) founded his first training business, a retail security labour force firm, at the age of 23, working in his mother's spare room. His entrepreneurship is supported by a strong work ethic and working with and understanding people from all walks of life. That, he believes is the key to his naturalness in identifying opportunities. He is enthusiastic about education and how to make people job ready for the future.

> From primary school I had my own little businesses ... [...] ... I didn't really find my niche in school. So when everyone went to university, I travelled the world for a few years. For me personally it was the best thing in my life: it took the blinkers off, I was relying on myself, building relationships, and I came back with a real thirst to want to succeed in something ... Mum was working as a covert loss prevention officer for Coles, apprehending shoplifters. Mum used to tell me the stories, so then I put my first business together, which was how to educate businesses in reducing shoplifting—it was called *National Loss Prevention*. Then I got a phone call from the Manager of the Franklins Supermarkets, I met up with him, and he asked me a defining question 'Do you provide covert loss prevention officers?' And I looked at him and I said 'Yes, I do'. So what do you do when you get into a bit of a pickle? I rang mum! And that was the beginning of our journey with *National Loss Prevention*. Within two and a half years I had hundreds of staff, we became the largest retail provider of coverts across Australia, just from that one question. Then I got into uniformed security. All my uniformed security were on the doors of Coles, Woolworths. I was about 24-25. I sold it to Wilson Parking, which is now Wilson Security, and it's still going, which I am proud of. That was my first entrepreneurial journey, and I actually call that my university degree. I learnt everything from running a business, responsibility, marketing, it was own personal MBA. Life is like chapters, and that for me was the end of that chapter ... [...] I then went into education, and chose workforce education, and that was the day I started *Franklyn Scholar*, at the end of 2007. I wanted to have an influence on something that I am passionate about, build something that is substantial. And I thought 'Well, I am just going to go for it!' So I surrounded myself with some fantastic advisors, put together a plan, went to the banks around looking at workforce education in Australia, saying that it wasn't meeting the needs of business, that there was no one national player in Australia, and it was such a cottage industry .... Westpac came on as shareholder ... And we started the *Franklyn Scholar* story.... [...]. So what is my next venture? I have come back into education, and this time,

looking along the lines of what will be the top industries in 2030, and where are universities positioning themselves, and I guess the real big question in education is: are we providing people that are job ready in the areas that are most needed? I found that in the creative industries—digital, design—your portfolio is more important... So the challenge is how do we provide accreditation, but how do we bring industry closer to influence curriculum? So I now have new colleges of digital design and entrepreneurship. We will bring industry into our faculty, we'll be educating in the agencies' work spaces.... We are creating colleges where industry and students are already mixing, with real job outcomes. We're very excited by that!

## 2.2 The Case Studies in This Book

This book comprises case studies of seven entrepreneurs in Australia who have established independent educational organisations that are also businesses, in one or a number of niche areas, ranging from fashion design to jazz music, photography, foundation studies, etc. The entrepreneurs, their educational organisations and range of course offerings are listed in Table 2.1.

The entrepreneurs are the founders or co-founders of the tertiary educational institutions, who continue to work in the role of managing director/director/CEO. Institutions deliver a range of vocational education and training (VET), and/or higher education (HE) qualifications, with some registered as dual sector institutions (VET/HE), offering the full range of tertiary qualifications, from accredited certificates to bachelor degrees, and postgraduate qualifications. Most institutions teach and train both local and international students.

Each case study presented in this book comprises:

- Background of the educational venture
- The entrepreneurial journey of the founder
- A profile of the entrepreneur behind the venture

Case studies consist of 'a detailed investigation, often with data collected over a period of time, of phenomena, within their context,' with the aim 'to provide an analysis of the context and processes which illuminate the theoretical issues being studied' (Hartley, 2004, p. 323).

Multiple case studies, such as those presented in this book, provide rich, real-world examples of experiences and perceptions that enable the reconstruction of reality and are an important and useful way of exploring and explaining patterns that may arise over time; they are 'discrete experiments that serve as replications, contrasts, and extensions to the emerging theory' (Yin, 1994).

Interviews are generally the most efficient way to gather information for case studies. The interviews conducted with the entrepreneurs in this book form the basis of their story, which consists of narrative interspersed with quotations.

The study of narratives is a widely accepted approach in social science (Polkinghorne, 1991). This approach is particularly suited to examine the background and personality of entrepreneurs from a behavioural perspective, as

## 2.2 The Case Studies in This Book

**Table 2.1** Entrepreneurs in the independent tertiary sector who participated in the study

| Name of entrepreneur | Name of educational institution/organisation | Area of offerings |
|---|---|---|
| Cass, Martin | JMC Academy (Sydney, Melbourne and Brisbane) | VET and Higher Education—Contemporary music and performance, audio engineering and sound production, digital design, entertainment business management, game development, 3D animation, film and TV production, song writing, VET and pathways |
| Jacobson, Mathew | Origin Human Resources (sold to Talent2), Ducere Global Business School (Melbourne, with online delivery across Australia and internationally) | VET and Higher Education—Business, management, entrepreneurship |
| Jones, Rod | Navitas (28 countries: Australia, UK, USA, Canada, New Zealand, Singapore, Sri Lanka, Indonesia, Kenya) | Foundation Studies programs into VET and Higher Education—Health and community services, business and management, public safety, IT, creative media English, IELTS, business production, careers and internship |
| Moss, Julie | Photography Studies College (Melbourne) | VET and Higher Education—Photography |
| Russo, Sarina | Sarina Russo Group (Queensland and Victoria, delivery across Australia, UK) | VET and Higher Education—Education, training, recruitment and job creation, business, business administration, warehousing, hospitality, retail |
| Quigley, Greg | Jazz Music Institute (Brisbane) | VET and Higher Education—Jazz music |
| Whitehouse, Leanne | Whitehouse Institute of Design (Sydney and Melbourne) | VET and Higher Education—Fashion design, interior design and styling |

suggested by Gartner (1989), in order to explore what entrepreneurs do to create organisations and why. Their personal narrative accounts reveal the choices they made and their perceptions of their entrepreneurial experiences (Berger & Luckmann, 1967).

The contributors to this book were asked to recount their stories of how they became educational entrepreneurs, by focusing and reflecting on their motivations, goals and individual experiences. By telling their stories and presenting them as their 'real, lived experiences', they reconstruct their reality, as they perceived it at the time. In sharing these rich, insightful personal stories, the readers will be able to focus on the role of the entrepreneur 'as prime actor' (Rae, 2000).

By exploring entrepreneurs' stories, this book adds considerable knowledge about entrepreneurship and specific qualitative knowledge of how people become entrepreneurs and how they develop entrepreneurial capabilities and behaviour.

# References

Berger, P. L., & Luckmann, T. (1967). *The social construction of reality. A treatise in the sociology of knowledge.* Garden City, NY: Anchor Books Doubleday.

Carter, N. M., Gartner, W. B., Shaver, K. G., & Gatewood, E. J. (2003). The career reasons of nascent entrepreneurs. *Journal of Business Venturing, 18*(1), 13–39.

Douglas, E. J., & Shepherd, D. A. (2002). Self-employment as a career choice: Attitudes, entrepreneurial intentions, and utility maximization. *Entrepreneurship Theory and Practice, 26*(3), 81–90.

Gartner, W. B. (1989). Some suggestions for research on entrepreneurial traits and characteristics. *Entrepreneurship Theory and Practice, 14*(1), 27–38.

Hartley, J. (2004). Case study research. In C. Cassell & G. Symon (Eds.), *Essential guide to qualitative methods in organizational research* (pp. 323–333). London: Sage.

Hills, G., Shrader, R., & Lumpkin, T. (1999). Opportunity recognition as a creative process. In P. D. Reynolds, W. D. Bygrave, S. Manigart, C. M. Mason, G. D. Meyer, H. J. Sapienza, et al. (Eds.), *Frontiers of entrepreneurship research* (pp. 216–227). Wellesley, MA: Babson College.

Hirschi, A., & Fischer, S. (2013). Work values as predictors of entrepreneurial career intentions. *Career Development International, 18*(3), 216–231.

Kirzner, I. M. (1979). *Perception, opportunity, and profit.* Chicago, IL: University of Chicago Press.

Lee, S. Y., Florida, R., & Acs, Z. J. (2004). Creativity and entrepreneurship: A regional analysis of new firm formation. *Regional Studies, 38*(8), 879–891.

Polkinghorne, D. E. (1991). Narrative and self-concept. *Journal of Narrative and Life History, 1*(2), 135–153.

Rae, D. (2000). Understanding entrepreneurial learning: A question of how? *International Journal of Entrepreneurial Behavior and Research, 6*(3), 145–159.

Shane, S. (2003). *A general theory of entrepreneurship: The individual-opportunity nexus.* Northampton, MA: Edward Elgar Publishing.

Shane, S., & Venkataraman, S. (2000). The promise of entrepreneurship as a field of study. *Academy of Management Review, 25*(1), 217–226.

Yin, R. K. (1994). *Case study research design and methods: Applied social research and methods series.* Thousand Oaks, CA: Sage.

Zanakis, S. H., Renko, M., & Bullough, A. (2012). Nascent entrepreneurs and the transition to entrepreneurship: Why do people start new businesses? *Journal of Developmental Entrepreneurship, 17*(1), 1–25.

Zhao, H., & Seibert, S. E. (2006). The big five personality dimensions and entrepreneurial status: A meta-analytical review. *Journal of Applied Psychology, 91*(2), 259–271.

# Part II
# Case Studies

# Dr Martin Cass: JMC Academy

## 3.1 About JMC

Established in 1982 by John Martin Cass, JMC Academy was originally founded in Sydney to meet the demand for qualified professionals in the entertainment technology industry. From day one, JMC Academy broke ground as Australia's first private college to qualify for accreditation in the fields of audio engineering, digital television and digital multimedia.

More than 30 years later, JMC Academy remains one of Australia's leading creative industries institutions, offering diplomas and degrees in music, song writing, audio engineering, film and television production, entertainment business management, digital design, 3D animation and game design.

With advanced-design campuses, ongoing technology upgrades, a dedicated team of academics and industry professionals and a network of international master class lecturers, JMC Academy is committed to ensuring its graduates make their own indelible mark on industry.

JMC Academy's ultimate focus is to deliver inspiring and technologically sophisticated programs, which cater to the global needs of the creative industries. It nurtures, supports and mentors students who share a true passion and dedication for these industries, and it guides them into rewarding careers.

According to Martin Cass, founder and Managing Director of JMC (Fig. 3.1), its uniqueness is defined by its people: 'It is defined by the individuality, distinct talents, personal histories, and achievements of each of our lecturers, and of each and every one of our students. It is the way these all interact to create the unique dynamics and superior outcomes delivered in every course' (JMC website).

JMC is the only Australian partner of the international network for the Berklee College of Music. They collaborate on joint initiatives including master classes presented by Berklee staff.

Students are mainly local, with approximately 7% international students who come from 35 different countries.

JMC has campuses in Brisbane, South Melbourne and Sydney's Ultimo.

**Fig. 3.1** Dr Martin Cass
(Photo courtesy of JMC)

## 3.2 The Entrepreneurial Journey Begins

From a very young age Martin Cass had always been interested in music and musical equipment. He was the guy at school who could always make the PA system work for the principal, whereas no one else could. To him, there was a logic about it, it came as second nature, he couldn't understand how people found it so difficult. He was totally fascinated by music and how to get music out to the public.

Martin's background is in audio engineering, specifically in music production, producing live sound for touring acts, and ultimately taking bands into recording studios. In 1980, he was doing front-of-house audio sound for a number of major Australian acts such as John English, Marcia Hines and Divinyls.

> In those days the act would want the front of house engineer, the person mixing the live sound, to go into the recording studio with them because that person had the experience of how to get 'their' sound. Well, that happened to me a lot.

He found a studio in Elizabeth Street, Surrey Hills, in Sydney that happened to have the appropriate equipment and charge reasonable rates. He was taking a lot of acts into this studio regularly to record them, so that they could send off their recordings to record companies, to do preproduction work, or release their final product. Martin soon realised that he never saw other clients in this facility, and whenever he needed to make a booking, it was always available, which he thought was odd. The owner explained that he was winding down the business as he was leaving, going overseas. In fact the business was for sale. Martin was intuitive and spontaneous, able to make decisions quickly, on a hunch, confident in his ability to seize an opportunity irrespective of the resources available. This decision would prove critical to his later success.

> So, being young, and reasonably smart, I took some time to think about it ... and in about 30 seconds I said 'I'll buy it!' So I went away, and decided that the only way I could buy this place was to sell everything I owned ... I went to a bank and I borrowed money, and I thought 'That was easy!' So I went to another bank, and said 'I have this amount of money,

and I want to borrow more', and they gave it to me, and I did that three times. I found out about ten years later that that wasn't legal! But that was what I did. I was young, and full of enthusiasm and arrogance and ego, why would I be scared? I didn't know what that meant. I had no concerns whatsoever...

Martin, his then wife Elizabeth (who passed away in 2002), together with their German shepherd Maya, were a young couple with a business and a large loan, so they set up a room in the studio, which became an office which doubled as a bedroom. Martin looked after production, Liz looked after the accounts and Maya, the German shepherd, looked after security. On their very first night at the studio, there was a knock on the door, and with Maya in Martin's hot pursuit down the stairs, he opened the front door to find four young men, about 16 years old, standing there, saying 'We are here for a class, and who are you?', explaining that they had paid in advance for one-to-one classes in audio production. The previous owner was now gone, so Martin felt morally bound to follow through and deliver. Together they looked through the notes, loosely called the curriculum, and it was obvious to him that it was back-to-front, all in the wrong order. To Martin it made really simple logic. So on that very first night, they took those notes and burnt them ... and JMC was founded.

And that's how JMC began, an accident, a giant but happy accident. There was no conscious decision to start a school, it just happened. And I taught those four, I worked with them, and I nurtured them and helped them through. I was not much older than they were, I was about 24 ... The four became eight, and eight turned into sixteen, and they kept coming, kept talking to friends.

Martin was learning on the job, quickly gaining knowledge and an understanding of the vocational education sector as well as the new business. Unbeknown to Martin, in 1982 Liz registered a business name, JMC Academy, using Martin's initials, John Martin Cass. Liz could clearly see the new path that Martin and his business were taking (Figs. 3.2 and 3.3).

Liz at the time understood me better than I understood myself ... I was supposed to be doing production, but over the previous six months I had done a lot less production and a lot more teaching, so clearly that's what I was going to do.

## 3.3 The Education Business Grows

Martin had no doubts about the future direction the media industry was taking and became alert to the opportunities that would open up if he developed his business in the same direction. Martin followed his hunch and expanded the music education aspect of the business into music production and digital television production.

Understanding the technology is so important ... I could see clear as day that as technology was improving with desktop computers, it was pretty obvious that what was then multimedia

**Fig. 3.2** Martin Cass in the early days of JMC (Photo courtesy of JMC)

was going to blossom, and moving away from having to take product or briefs to an advertising agency as people would be able to do it in-house. Most of that kind of production work now is done in-house because the technology is easily available. To me it was a no brainer. Where else was it going to go?

In the mid 1990s the state-based regulators were created. This gave Martin an opportunity to accredit the programs he was delivering to students, and to formally recognise JMC Academy as the provider of vocational education in the creative industry fields. JMC Academy's course was one of the earliest to be registered.

> JMC was the first provider to be accredited to deliver the audio engineering program, the first accredited to deliver the digital television program—this is when digital television was really new—and digital animation. We were ahead of the game on many fronts.

Over the years, Martin has heavily invested in cutting-edge music and television technology for the college, in the latest equipment, recording studios, rehearsal rooms, film and television studios with green screen, animation and games labs, film and TV edit suites as well as auditoriums.

3.4 A Team Effort

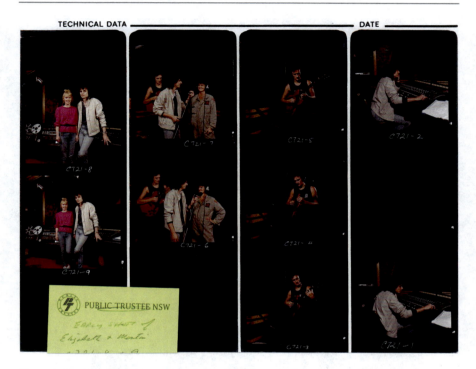

**Fig. 3.3** Promotional photo shoot at JMC's original studios in Surrey Hills, Sydney, including Martin Cass and late wife Elizabeth, with JMC staff (Photo courtesy of JMC)

## 3.4 A Team Effort

Martin's role in the college has gradually transformed. In the initial stages, he coped with, rather than controlled his business venture. It grew spontaneously, with Martin moving from one role to another as he saw the need.

> If you consider the whole history of the college, every 5 to 10 years, it changed, and my role also changed. Initially I was doing music production, then I was teaching and doing music production, then it became teaching and running a college. When our program suddenly became accredited, my role shifted away from fully running the college as it became too big a job for one person; I needed a manager and others, and I began to focus more on where we were going rather than how we were going to get there.

He attributes part of his early success to his then wife, Elizabeth.

> At the time, Liz understood me better than I understood myself, and she helped the process to mature. [...] Liz passed away just when the business had got to a certain point where it could roll a lot more easily, and she missed all the positive things that came after that.

**Fig. 3.4** Dr Martin Cass and Dr George Markakis graduating with a Professional Doctorate in Industry and Professions, University of New England (Photo courtesy of JMC)

Over the years, as the business has grown, Martin has put great effort in building a strong and long-lasting management team. He believes that one of the most common mistakes that an organisation makes is in regard to weak management staff who have poor skills particularly in finance and human resources. A teaching institute is, after all, a business that needs to be financially viable. Martin has very high regard for his management staff, in particular for his CEO, Dr George Markakis, who has been with JMC for over 20 years and has supported him professionally and personally through every stage (Fig. 3.4).

> George understands not just me but what we do, how we do it and why we do it. That is very important because I can rely on him to understand the why, which is very important because that gets back to not thinking about JMC just as a business but as a culture, as a way of thinking.

## 3.4 A Team Effort

Martin has successfully recruited staff who maintain strong links with industry and are long standing and loyal. The staff are committed to their industry, the college, the curriculum and the students. They are experts in their field and passionate about JMC and about passing on their knowledge and skills to students within an educational environment. They share his vision and his passion and strive for excellence in their work and in making their innovative contribution. Gradually he has built a team of like-minded and cohesive managers, staff and employees (Fig. 3.5).

> Our uniqueness is defined by our people. It is defined by the individuality, distinct talents, personal histories, and achievements of each of our lecturers, and of each and every one of our students. It is the way these all interact to create the unique dynamics and superior outcomes delivered in every course. [...] I think about the people who have been here for so long. So many of them have been here for a long time, some for well over 15 years. I think about the marriages that have come out of the organisation over the years, which is nice. I think about some of the people who have moved on and done fantastic things; graduates and staff have left and done their own things, done exceptionally well. I think about some of the great people we've had here who aren't with us anymore. Ian Miller who was just a fantastic educator; he just had a knack of getting the information across, he was brilliant and a brilliant/fantastic producer. Bob Dickson, who was a great engineer, he could hear things that you wouldn't hear it, I wouldn't hear it and he could pick it out and show you why it works and how it affected the listener. And many others.

This has enabled Martin to take on a more defined leadership role and spend precious time on aspects of the business in which he has more expertise and technical know-how, identifying and evaluating new opportunities, and making new deals.

> It's not my role to run the organisation; that's George's role. My role is to provide the direction and stay in touch with the direction, and make sure the 'who we are' and 'why we exist' is constantly reaffirmed and people understand it. I stay on top of the technology to a certain degree. There are also other people here who talk to me about what the technology is doing and I learn from them. That's really important. As long as we keep communicating and understanding where we need to go, how can we go wrong?

Martin is confident and optimistic: this is underpinned by a large degree of expertise, hard work and diligence, which has enabled JMC Academy to grow into one of the most successful educational providers in media production in Australia. He knows that it is risky to fall behind in the two rapidly changing and uncertain environments in which he works across—media and education—and he understands that one of the challenges he constantly faces is that he must often act quickly, make fast and risky decisions in order to exploit innovation and achieve new goals and at the same time abide by the strict compliance requirements imposed by the tertiary education regulators ASQA (for vocational education) and TEQSA (for higher education).

**Fig. 3.5** L to R: Dr Martin Cass (Managing Director) and wife Heather, and Dr George Markakis (CEO) with Karen Markakis (Director of Marketing) at the official opening of JMC's second campus in Brisbane in 2017 (Photo courtesy of JMC)

## 3.5   JMC Grows

Martin is confident about growth opportunities in the business of education.

> I feel very good about delivering a body of knowledge to people. I am open to the opportunity, and I am happy to deliver—it's as simple as that. I suppose it allowed me to

continue doing what I did very well, which was production, but it also allowed me the opportunity to develop something that I became even better at, and that is teaching.

Martin's focus and passion is in educating and skilling, and giving back to the students.

> To be truthful, and forgive me for sounding overconfident, but I have always had the ability to get the information across, and help people understand in very simple terms why something is the way it is, and how to achieve results. I had that knack at school; I was always the guy that could make it work. It was second nature, and my whole attitude of it being very simple rubbed off on people and they accepted things being simple. It's all about how you do it.

In balancing profits and education, Martin combines the educator side of himself (his passion) with running a business (a service-based focus). He is aware that financial viability plays a major role, but his focus is on delivering quality education and training programs. He believes they are quite balanced.

> I am happy with the profit I am making and I will continue to deliver quality. Profit is important but it is not the be all and end all. The reality is that there are many private providers who operate ethically.

Martin remains staunchly dedicated to lifting the quality of education and training in the creative industries, as well as in the overall private education sector. He was the National Chair of the Australian Council for Private Education and Training (ACPET),[1] the national association representing private providers of tertiary education, from September 2011 to August 2015 as well as the Director representing NSW from 2008 to August 2015. He is aware that a number of players have come into the sector, sadly not all with the right intentions.

> Education needs to be the primary purpose. I find it frustrating that some players come in specifically because it's a good business model rather than because they have a passion for the industry. Most have come into private education because that's the industry that they worked in or were teaching in, wanting to add to the value or to the quality of our education system, so there is a passion for it.

Being closely linked to the industry in which he works, he learned early that one of the most essential requirements for any educational business is that it is delivering what the clients need, and not necessarily what the clients want. Therefore, it is important to work closely with the rapidly changing industry and understand what the industry needs from graduates (Fig. 3.6).

> What the clients want certainly plays a significant role, but what they will need for their future work is even more important, which of course is related to what industry needs in

---

[1] Formed in 1992, the Australian Council for Private Education and Training (ACPET) was renamed the Independent Tertiary Education Council Australia (ITECA) in May 2019.

**Fig. 3.6** JMC students and staff (Photo courtesy of JMC)

terms of its employees. If you are addressing those issues, then of course your graduates will have the skills to gain employment. Communicate with the industry, that's an absolute must, the industry for which you are providing the graduates.

Martin is passionate about his work, his students and his college. He is committed to nurturing, supporting and mentoring students who share real enthusiasm and dedication for the creative multimedia industries.

> I believe in what I'm doing, and when you believe in what you're doing, it just lunges out to everybody! [...] It's about the culture. It's what we do and who we are. People try to copy it and some are very good at it but at the end of the day, you never have two cultures that are exactly the same. Only one will win hearts and minds. The other will win minds but few hearts and I think that's a significant difference. That shows with our alumni for example, with the animation—if you go anywhere in the world, you will find graduates who have done work even way back in 1983/84 when they completed their qualifications, who went off and did so well. It's such a buzz when you look on the wall outside and see their names. That's it, it's the only thing I really enjoy. There are other things I enjoy but I enjoy that 'the most'. I was on a plane recently and the flight attendant came to me and said 'You probably don't remember me. I was a student at JMC and I graduated two years ago. I just want to let you know that I'm working part time as a flight attendant and I'm on my way to New York as I have some musical work to do there.' That's what you live for, that's the thing.

## 3.6  Martin Cass: The Entrepreneur

Martin's music background and experience played a major role in supporting his early entrepreneurial ventures—he found himself within a context where resources and opportunities met, and multiplied.

> I was working with a fellow by the name of Alan Caswell; he was a great songwriter. We were producing lots of artists. I was engineering and he was doing the musical production, together as a team. We came up with the idea of this fellow called Don Spencer who was doing Play School on the ABC and why shouldn't these young kids be educated using music? Why not? So we did. We taught kids through music and we created a range of other programs.

Entrepreneurship often derives from the need for change. Martin was focused on the need to expand his activity in the music scene.

> I was young, and full of enthusiasm and arrogance and ego. I had no concerns whatsoever, because in my mind, all that was going to happen was that I was going to bring more work into that particular studio, just as I had been . . . I am open to new ideas, and happy to accept change.

Martin was driven by the opportunity he could see, embracing the risks in his path.

> I think people miss those opportunities because they are blinded by either their own insecurities or they focus on what they do and they can't see that there are other ways . . .

Like other successful entrepreneurs, Martin speaks of an intangible instinct or 'gut feeling' about the potential underlying success of an opportunity at hand.

> When you are young, you tend to do things instinctively, and as you get older you tend to analyse and analyse. And periodically I have to say to myself 'OK, you're not sure, and you are analysing. Just use your instinct.' And that works for me. There are times when you speak to people who will say something won't work, and you feel instinctively that there's plenty of reasons why it should. At the end of the day, have a shot at the goal. What's the worst thing that can happen? You may miss, and if you miss, well, you'll know not to do it next time!

Martin accepts that there are always risks in the big decisions at hand. He admits he feels uncomfortable with high risk situations when the outcome is unknown.

> I'm not sure doubt is the right word; I think fear is the more honest word. Because you do get afraid but that doesn't mean you don't act. You're just be a bit more careful about how you use your instinct and the decisions that you are making, because now it impacts on many more people. In 1982, it impacted only on two.

> Before I make a decision, the fear is whether it will be the right one and you're working again on analysis and instinct. When you overanalyse to the point where you're getting confused, then you resort to instinct. I believe that it's human nature that as you get older, you tend to

have less fight instinct and more fear instinct. People call that wisdom. You are reacting less and thinking more. But once I make a decision, I don't doubt myself on it, I just go ahead and do it.

He is more comfortable about taking measured and considered risks, something he has learnt through a few failed ventures.

In 1994, an opportunity became available to open up in Melbourne. I went ahead with it and took the facility over and sent some people down. However, I underestimated the complication of having two locations to deal with, and didn't understand that it was the right people that had to be there to run it because I wasn't there.

The venture failed because I was too young and inexperienced, too focused on actually delivering myself rather than having other people to deliver and allow myself an opportunity to look at the bigger picture. So my failure was that I didn't understand what it actually took. My success was being smart enough to recognise it, to stop what I was doing and close it down, bring those people back and employ them in Sydney, and take a step back and wait and think and absorb and gain experience. All those things became instinct, because in early 2000, I took over a space in this building and did it all over again but without the same problems.

In retrospect, Martin views failures only as temporary setbacks. He has also learnt to rely more on his instincts.

At the time I focused on the failure, because nobody likes failing. I know I wasn't listening to my instinct at that time because all along I kept thinking that something wasn't right but I still had a go at it anyway. I should have listened to my gut feeling, something was not quite right, and I should have walked away. Frankly, I had the wrong people.

Looking at JMC now, and the success he has attained, Martin is proud of what he has achieved.

I'm proud of the fact that I look at it and say "Wow! Yeah, it is pretty big". Sometimes I get fearful or doubtful because... how long can it stay like that? Will it keep growing? Who knows?!

## Reference

JMC Academy. (n.d.). Accessed February 10, 2019, from https://www.jmcacademy.edu.au/

# 4. Mathew Jacobson: Ducere Global Business School

## 4.1 About Ducere Global Business School

Ducere is an innovative education provider of high-quality tertiary leadership programs. The word Ducere, from the Latin, means 'to lead' or 'to guide'—this is the philosophy of the Ducere Global Business School, where leadership, entrepreneurship and education are fundamentally connected. Ducere, along with its partners, aims to bridge the gap between real industry leadership and rigorous academic guidance to deliver unique enterprise skills for the twenty-first-century innovation economy.

As part of the Ducere Group, the Ducere Global Business School is an online education provider that partners with established universities and innovative organisations, businesses and global leaders to be the most student-focused and industry-relevant business school in Australia. In 2017, Ducere, in partnership with the University of Canberra, was named a finalist in the Australian Financial Review Higher Education Awards for offering 'Australia's most innovative MBA' (Financial Review) and 'the most unique MBA in the world ... focusing on real industry problems' (The Australian newspaper).

> Ducere and the University of Canberra have come together to produce this ground-breaking MBA, delivered nationally online and provides students with the opportunity to solve real business problems as part of their learning.

Ducere offers higher education that is flexible, practical, industry-relevant and innovation-focused. It delivers highly engaging, industry-focused higher education programs responding to current and future needs of industry—bachelor degrees in business, marketing or entrepreneurship, an MBA in business and a Graduate Certificate in Business Administration offered through flexible and self-directed online study, focusing on real-world business projects and dynamic industry events. Students work on practical business plans and project case studies and develop

© Springer Nature Switzerland AG 2020
L. Hougaz, *Entrepreneurs Creating Educational Innovation*,
https://doi.org/10.1007/978-3-030-28655-2_4

critical know-how and entrepreneurial skillsets required for success in an economy transformed by innovation.

> The MBA is integrated with Ducere's global faculty, comprised of hundreds of world leaders from Presidents and past Prime Ministers, to Nobel Prize winners; has no exams and embeds projects with organisations including NAB, KPMG, SEEK and the Federal Government amongst others [...] The MBA is a project-based curriculum in which students apply everything learnt to real-world situations and practical business challenges. Being immersed in the MBA's challenges and working within team environments and industry partners, students will develop important commercial skills they can apply and deliver in their professional and commercial endeavours.

Ducere has partnerships with Monash University (South Africa), the University of Wales (the oldest university in the UK after Oxford and Cambridge) and the national university of Namibia.

Ducere's innovative higher education programs support educational and leadership programs in 21 African nations through the work of the Ducere Foundation.

## 4.2 The Ducere Foundation

Ducere is a social enterprise that delivers pioneering education initiatives in Australia and Africa. Mathew Jacobson is founder of the Ducere Foundation (Figs. 4.1 and 4.2). Primarily funded through the work of the Ducere Global Business School in Australia and Mauritius, the Foundation works in close partnerships with sovereign states, major universities, philanthropic leaders and major businesses to deliver educational programs across 21 African nations, including Botswana, Rwanda, South Africa and Kenya. Mathew collaborates with local governments and schools, and partners with many not-for-profit organisations, to improve the quality of public education in Africa.

**Fig. 4.1** Mathew Jacobson (Photo courtesy of Mathew Jacobson, Ducere)

## 4.2 The Ducere Foundation

**Fig. 4.2** Mathew Jacobson with the Executive Director of Ducere Foundation, Di Fleming (Photo courtesy of Mathew Jacobson, Ducere)

Mathew has always been interested in working with at-risk children, keeping them at school, engaged in education.

> I am a big believer in not giving people a handout, and not giving people food coupons every day for the rest of their life. A much better solution is to give people an education, a career path of vocation, help them get them a job, and enable them to stand on their own feet. The best form of charity is to actually remove the need for charity. That is something that I've always been very passionate about, and a strong philosophy for me personally.

The foundation supplies teachers and provides school uniforms, books and teaching programs. It funds ground-breaking publishing, school development and mentorship projects, providing unique learning and leadership opportunities across the African countries (Fig. 4.3).

> One of the challenges for any not-for-profit organisation is raising the funding to run its programs: they typically spend most of their time getting money as opposed to delivering the great work that they want to be doing. I didn't really want to be doing that, so it was very important to create a model which is self-funded and self-sustainable. That in itself is an exciting initiative.

**Fig. 4.3** Mathew Jacobson with former Australian Prime Minister, Hon Julia Gillard, visiting a primary school in Zambia (Photo courtesy of Mathew Jacobson, Ducere)

> We have all our own staff locally on the ground in Africa, teachers, mentors, we run food programs, provide school uniforms, books, teaching programs, all funded through the academic programs of Ducere.

The Ducere Foundation employs staff locally in Africa who aim to engage and motivate learners and passionate leaders, preparing them for a successful future. The foundation works with local governments and communities across Africa capturing children's stories, building pride in oral tradition and creating leadership opportunities through publishing, school development and mentorship initiatives. It empowers the voices of children through sustainable and scalable philanthropic projects. Mathew is grateful in his life to have had the chance to complete his own studies and strongly believes that education is a right for every child in the world.

Since 2013, the Ducere Foundation's *Read Out Loud* radio program has been broadcasting from Livingstone, Zambia, across southern Africa through Mosi-O-Tunya Radio, giving hundreds of children the opportunity to share their life experience, discuss their ideas across the airwaves and stimulate rich conversation within their communities.

The *African Children's Stories* project has documented and amplified the voices of 10,500 students in over 21 African nations and published over 700,000 collections of traditional stories since 2014 (Fig. 4.4). It also provides resources and master

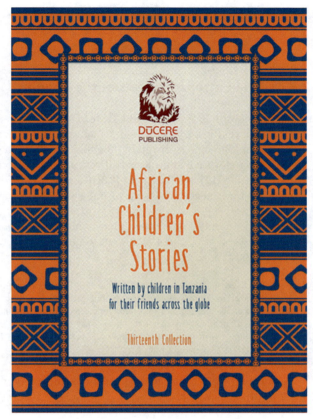

**Fig. 4.4** Ducere Foundation publication, *The 13th Collection from Tanzania*, includes stories from children in the Hai District, Kilimanjaro Region, Northern Tanzania. *The proceeds of the sale of these books is 100% invested in the publication and distribution of more books into the hands of children across Africa.* https://ducerefoundation.org/african-children-stories/ (Photo courtesy of Mathew Jacobson, Ducere)

classes through the *School Improvement* program to improve student outcomes, particularly in mathematics, science and English. Education is seen as the key driver of meaningful social change, especially across Africa, where rapid urbanisation is providing both opportunities and challenges. The Ducere *Peace Education* program delivers curriculum content and mentorship through debating, human rights practice, peace building, advocacy and leadership.

In 2016, the Mauritian collection of the Ducere *African Children's Stories* project was launched in Moka by the Mauritian Minister of Education and Human Resources, Tertiary Education and Scientific Research, Mrs Leela Devi Dookun Luchoomun, and Mrs Julia Gillard, Ducere Chancellor, and former Prime Minister of Australia.

In 2018, Mathew Jacobson launched a new foundation called *P.O.W.E.R.— Protection of Wo/Men's Economic Rights*, Australia's first organisation dedicated specifically to increasing awareness of economic abuse in domestic violent relationships. Its aim is to educate by empowering women and men to utilise financial literacy skills and strategies and develop programs in schools that promote financial literacy and empowerment.

## 4.3 The Entrepreneurial Journey Begins

Mathew Jacobson is Founder and CEO of Ducere. He is a graduate in law and arts and more recently has specialised in the area of leadership. He is a long-time entrepreneur who enjoys disrupting the higher education landscape, creating some of the most innovative and successful educational platforms and projects (Redrup, 2013; White, 2015). He has established three tertiary education businesses, two property investment companies in Australia and the USA and a technology incubator in Melbourne.

Mathew's family were immigrants with humble beginnings. None of them completed secondary school, nor went to university; instead they established their own small business.

> I was exposed to business from a young age. Everyone in my family set up their own businesses, all my uncles, my dad, my grandfather. It was a culture that I grew up in. No one worked in an accounting firm, no one worked as an engineer, no one had employed roles. They were all business owners. That was a great driver of entrepreneurialism in my family. I started businesses in grade one. I'd have the principal saying 'This is not acceptable, you can't be running businesses out of school!'

Mathew had a very unstable education as his family often moved house, and he was forced to change schools.

> It was a challenge to get good schooling, I never really had an interest in education or reading or learning. Also by the time I was 15 and 16, I was pretty much living independently. What that meant was that I had a very undisciplined approach to education. I was not the sort of person who was organised, prepared and did my homework. (Mathew Jacobson, in Financial Review)

Thanks to an English teacher who inspired and motivated him, Mathew completed his secondary schooling and went on to study at Monash University in Melbourne, and Bond University in Queensland majoring in arts and law.

> Even though I studied literature, philosophy and law, I had no intention of ever being a lawyer. I knew that I wanted to be in business and have a more creative outlet. Philosophical discussions are more about debate and opinion rather than right or wrong and I really enjoyed that critical thinking and analysis. That was very, very exciting. It was an area of university education that really appealed to me .... Law, management and marketing, I found to be very artificial. I found them to be very textbook-based, outdated and theoretical. I felt that the lecturers didn't really have practical expertise. For me, with a passion for education, I was always thinking about what could be done to fix that problem. (Mathew Jacobson, in Financial Review)

## 4.3 The Entrepreneurial Journey Begins

Mathew started his early career in law, working for various law firms in Australia, the USA and the UK. This gave him experience in the field, but more importantly for him, it was an opportunity to travel and gain a broader international experience.

> I worked a little overseas in the US and the UK as a lawyer, but it was more a good way to fund my travelling, not because I wanted or really ever saw a career in law.

Mathew returned to Melbourne in 1990 with a broader life experience and many new ideas to pursue. In 1998, he founded his first enterprise, HatchingIT, a technology incubator supporting tech start-ups in e-learning, digital media, digital analytics and Internet solutions. Recognising online training delivery as a source of potential value, HatchingIT partnered with Telstra, Compaq Computers, Sun Micro Systems, Telstra and the Victorian Government in Australia to offer compliance training online. His knowledge and experience in law supported his initiative.

> Utilising my law background, we started to offer compliance training online, which is great for companies because equal opportunity training, or safety training, is not something that really adds value to a business, they don't want to spend time or money on it, it's just a tick-the-box type of exercise, so they want to do it as efficiently as possible. That's the driver with compliance type training—it's policy, privacy, regulations, those sorts of things. E-learning is perfect for that because if you have a national workforce, having it all accessible online, all automatically tracked and recorded, is a very efficient way of doing it. So that's basically what we started doing.

The business gradually evolved, and in 2005 Mathew moved on to establish his next enterprise, Origin Human Resources, a firm that specialised in offering accredited training to large global financial institutions such as PriceWaterhouseCoopers, KPMG and Axa, Merrill Lynch Wealth Management, Goldman Sachs, banks and auto finance companies.

> Financial services training is a highly regulated industry, so I built a private training organisation that offered accredited training with formal certification. We worked all across Australia, partnering very large organisations with thousands of students a year. Some of the largest organisations were clients of ours.

The key to success, for Mathew, was having a quality product and online experience.

> We had a premier product. I definitely believe in going out with excellent quality that will put you in a leadership position. And no one in the market had the quality of online experience that we had.

The company was sold in 2011 to Talent2, a global publicly listed company.

## 4.4 From an Education Business to More than an Educational Enterprise

When Mathew sold his company in 2011, his initial thought was to simply work part-time and take time to do things he enjoyed doing. But that did not last long.

> And then I thought, what am I going to do? Because I wanted to do something not just for the purpose of working, but something that I was really interested in and passionate about.

Mathew established his next enterprise, 'Ducere', one with a difference, focused on two very distinct sides of education. One is academic education, effectively a fee-based business that offers full qualifications, and the other is a foundation, a self-sustainable and self-funded philanthropy funded entirely through the academic business.

The academic programs are offered by the Ducere Global Business School. 'Ducere' is the Latin word meaning 'to lead', and the Ducere Business School has a niche and very narrow focus, aiming to building a global brand of excellence in leadership across business, management and entrepreneurship. Its online learning program is delivered through documentary quality production.

> The important aspect that's different is the high level of quality and engagement. But the critical aspect for me and for our organisation is not the technology—to me technology is not the driver, it's the enabler. The critical thing with education is the content itself: what are you learning and who are you learning from?

Mathew's own experience at university taught him that academics mostly lack real professional work experience, and teach traditionally, from textbooks—he had identified a potential gap to exploit.

> One of the gaps that we see in the market, which is a stereotype and you hear about this often, is that you go to a typical business school anywhere in the world and you're going to be hearing from a lecturer who has probably never worked in a business in his or her life, you're going to take a marketing class from someone who probably never had a marketing job. You know, it's purely academic work. There's a role for academic learning, theory and the underpinning knowledge, but that's a part of the whole puzzle, it's not the solution to learning.

Ducere's academic program is developed and delivered by a faculty of global leaders such as former Australian Prime Minister John Howard, ex-Qantas Airways chief executive Margaret Jackson, Archbishop Desmond Tutu and other high-profile business leaders, Nobel Prize winners and CEOs. Mathew aims to work with the best (Fig. 4.5).

> If you do a course with Ducere, every element is delivered by a real world leader.
> Every single lesson, every unit is taught by a President, a Prime Minister, a self-made billionaire, a marketing expert. We have people like Nobel Prize winners, Harvard Professors, incredible people with diverse backgrounds from all over the world from Africa,

**Fig. 4.5** Mathew Jacobson meeting US President Bill Clinton in New York (Photo courtesy of Mathew Jacobson, Ducere)

Israel, Asia, America, and Europe. It's learning from real people who have created the most successful outcomes in their field whether it's science or politics or business.

Ducere provides a creative solution for universities and other higher education institutions all over the world that understand the need to complement their existing traditional courses with an online program with a difference. Mathew believes this model fills a gap in higher education.

> We believe the best form of education links formal tertiary education with real world experience.

Online learners studying business courses and MBAs in universities are linked with companies and world leaders who provide hands-on learning through the Ducere online programs. The students are given access to targeted interviews with a number of world leaders, focused specifically around their course topics. Seek founder Andrew Basset tells students about how to create a digital brand, while the interview with the entrepreneur and businessman Lindsay Fox is about how to get outcomes through negotiation.

> We think the best approach is a combination of academic learning, theory, and the underpinning knowledge that is offered by universities, with the real world experience. We partner with higher education institutions—we don't compete with them.

Ducere has identified its niche area, with a narrow focus and a globally recognised brand of business and management.

We've been developing relationships globally from day one. We've got a track record of getting the most successful and talented people in the world to be a part of what we're doing, we have fantastic technology, a brilliant platform for engaging learning materials, so that's what we want to focus on.

## 4.5   Mathew Jacobson: The Entrepreneur

Mathew has been inspired by entrepreneurs like Richard Branson (Fig. 4.6) and Blake Mycoskie, the founder of TOM Shoes (Shoes For Better Tomorrows). He admires their innovativeness and risk-taking attitude. Like them, Mathew has taken his share of risks, with no capital nor investors to sustain him, and has succeeded.

> When I started out, as a 20 year old, I had no money, no investors, no partners. 20 years ago I just had ideas and no one was really interested in investing money and supporting what we were trying to do. It's very hard to get money when you really need it. The irony is that when you sell companies and you get a level of success and people recognise you built a national company and been able to sell for a decent exit, then people and banks say 'yes we want to invest, we want to partner with you'. But now I don't need the money, I can just fund it myself.

Mathew enjoys looking at things in a positive, creative and interesting way and identifying opportunities and gaps in the marketplace.

> Entrepreneurial business is creative because you're coming up with new concepts, new ideas and new ways of doing things that haven't been done before.

**Fig. 4.6** Mathew Jacobson in company of entrepreneur Richard Branson on Necker Island (Photo courtesy of Mathew Jacobson, Ducere)

## 4.5 Mathew Jacobson: The Entrepreneur

A man of vision and intuition, Mathew recognises that he has the ability to spot opportunities at the 'right time'.

> I definitely do have the ability to see an opportunity and see a gap in the market, see something that hasn't been done before in a certain way, put a model together. It's really about coming up with a new, entrepreneurial idea and vision for a business that can be very successful. It's about the innovation, the idea, the creativity—that's what's excites me!

He is a naturally unstructured, adaptable and relatively undisciplined person. He recognises his deficiencies and ensures that he has the appropriate support.

> I don't believe I'm very good at anything in particular. I'm not good at operations, I'm not good at management, I'm not good at detail, I don't have discipline—that's an accurate description of myself. I'm aware of the things that I don't do well. I get bored easily. And that's fine. I'm aware of the things that I don't do well. And one of the things I believe causes a lot of businesses or entrepreneurs to fail is that they don't recognise their deficiencies, and that's a recipe for disaster. People typically aren't aware of their strengths and weaknesses. The most successful people in the world don't do everything, they know what they're good at and they know what they're not good at, and they get in the skills that they need.

Mathew needs to feel passionate about an idea or an issue. Only then he will feel enthusiastic and motivated to take on the challenge, and be highly committed to succeed.

> What drives me is the opportunity, and being excited about doing something creative and innovative. I'm only going to be able to stick with something if it's very engaging or interesting. I've got to constantly be excited and passionate about what I'm doing. Only then I can give it my best! What we are doing with Ducere has not really ever been done anywhere in the world before, it's exciting!

His entrepreneurial flair is underpinned by a strong personal vision, commitment and determination to empower access to education across the world. He is completely passionate about his goal which has become a priority in his life.

> The Ducere Business School and the Ducere Foundation—it's really like a symbiotic relationship, they're both equally as important to our organisation.
>
> I've always had a vision of how can we make the world a better place and do things to improve the lives of others. That's very exciting! What we're doing in Africa is completely entrepreneurial and innovative, it's never been done anywhere else in the world before. We build our own publishing houses, we are documenting the oral traditions across the continent, kids are learning in their own culture and their own learning, we're building peace centres in countries where issues of conflict and diversity have been problems for many years. We're helping to build a culture of tolerance and embracing diversity rather than seeing it as a negative. So on many levels it's a really exciting, and from an academic perspective how much more excitement can you get?!

Mathew is focused and driven to achieve. He is a great believer that taking a risk and having a go leads to success. He also believes that his entrepreneurial attitude and work can make a difference in the world—this is what drives him to continue.

I'd like to think I'm doing something new, ground breaking, you know, trying to create something that hasn't really been done. It doesn't have to be revolutionary; it may just be an incremental improvement. So in that sense then, definitely, I would say that's my role and that's my background. That's all I want to do.

Mathew is a highly regarded and esteemed entrepreneur. He is a regular media contributor on topics of business innovation and entrepreneurship, including Sky news and articles in *Wealth Creator*, *Marketing Magazine*, *Business First*, *Smart Magazine*, *Start-Up Smart* and *Business Builders*.

As a thought leader on innovation in education, Mathew has hosted and spoken at numerous academic and business events including chairing the 2014 ADC Forum Summit on 'the Future of Australian Higher Education', Harvard University, European governments, Startup Grind and Universities Australia, amongst others.

Mathew is professionally recognised as an innovative educational expert: he is a member of the ADC Education Taskforce; participant in the Victorian International Education Ministerial Advisory Roundtable; and member of the Clinton Global Initiative.

## References

Ducere Foundation. (n.d.). Accessed February 13, 2019, from https://ducerefoundation.org/
Ducere Global Business School. (n.d.). Accessed May 13, 2019, from https://www.ducere.edu.au/
Financial Review. (2016, April 1). Entrepreneur Mathew Jacobson tells how education changed his life. *Financial Review*. Accessed February 13, 2019, from http://www.afr.com/leadership/entrepreneur-mat-jacobson-tells-how-education-changed-his-life-20160331-gnuzsy
P.O.W.E.R. Foundation. (n.d.). Accessed November 20, 2018, from power.org.au
Redrup, Y. (2013). *An entrepreneur, a lawyer, and a philanthropist: Meet Ducere's founder Mat Jacobson*. Accessed February 13, 2019, from https://www.smartcompany.com.au/entrepreneurs/influencers-profiles/meet-ducere-s-founder-mat-jacobson/
White, S. (2015, May 27). Ducere CEO and entrepreneur Mathew Jacobson values education and a work ethic. *The Sydney Morning Herald*. Accessed September 19, 2018, from https://www.smh.com.au/business/ducere-ceo-and-entrepreneur-mathew-jacobson-values-education-and-a-work-ethic-20150521-gh6ujo.html

# Rod Jones: Navitas

## 5.1 About Navitas

Navitas was co-founded in Perth, Western Australia (WA), in 1994 by Rod Jones, a government and university administrator, and Dr Peter Larsen, a secondary education teacher and administrator. Having a good understanding of the Australian university sector, and the direction it was taking, they became interested in viable options for the growing international student market. Together, in 1994 they founded their initial venture, *Perth Institute of Business and Technology (PIBT)*, and began a long-term collaboration with Edith Cowan University.

Following the establishment of more colleges in collaboration with a number of universities in other major cities in Australia, in 2004 the two partners listed the first education company (*IBT Education*) in Australia on the stock exchange as a public company.

In 2007, IBT Education was rebranded *Navitas*. Gradually, Navitas has become a leading global education provider that delivers an extensive range of educational services to over 80,000 students annually through more than 120 institutions in 31 countries in North America, Europe, Africa, Asia and Australia.

With more than 55,000 international students, and around 6000 staff on its roll, Navitas delivers a broad range of university pathway programs, which provide more than two-thirds of its earnings, as well as health and social service education, creative media education, professional and industry placement, English language and migrant settlement services.

Its most successful program is the *Pathway Program* model offered to international students who enrol to study higher education courses outside their own country and who face the challenges of English as a second language, adapting to a new culture and a different education system. Navitas English language and pathway programs ensure that students are given the extra support and assistance needed to succeed at a higher education level. In Australia and the UK, domestic students are also able to enrol in Navitas colleges to take advantage of the supportive environment to enhance their academic potential. Students who successfully complete Navitas pathway programs and meet partner entry requirements are able to progress directly into the second-year programs at the partner university.

Navitas' pathway programs are taught on the partner university's campus. Students can access the university's libraries, computer laboratories, recreation facilities, common areas and other general student services as well as having access to student clubs and societies. This assists students to integrate into campus life in the first year through Navitas, making the transition to second year at the university much easier.

In 1994, Navitas began with one single university partnership with Edith Cowan University in Perth. Since then, it has expanded internationally, partnering with universities in Australia, the USA, Canada, the UK, Singapore, New Zealand and Sri Lanka, aligning with the partners' mission and goals.

## 5.2 The Entrepreneurial Journey Begins

Rod Jones (Fig. 5.1) readily admits that he was not a brilliant student himself, dropping out of the first year of an agriculture degree at university to work as a farm hand and later with the State Department of Agriculture. He then moved to work with the Commonwealth Government and returned to university on a part-time basis to complete a degree in commerce. His next roles were with the University of Western Australia and then the Tertiary Institutions Service Centre, the student

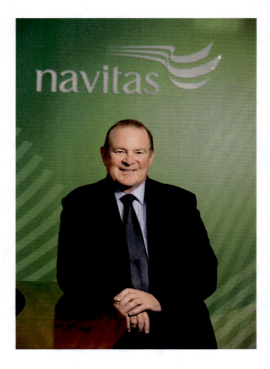

**Fig. 5.1** Rod Jones (Photo courtesy of Rod Jones, Navitas)

## 5.2 The Entrepreneurial Journey Begins

admission centre for the Western Australian universities. It was in that role that he was introduced to international education and was responsible for the establishment of the Western Australian senior school curriculum and examination system being offered outside Australia for the first time.

At the age of 37, Rod was appointed Deputy Director of the Secondary Education Authority.

> When I was appointed there was a lot of outcry from the educational community, but they deliberately brought me in for the way I thought, I was renowned for getting things done.

In 1986, the Australian Federal Labour Government, under the leadership of Prime Minister Bob Hawke, changed the rules to enable full-fee-paying international students to study at Australian universities. In early 1987, Rod was seconded by the then State Minister for Education who recognised that if Western Australia was ever going to be a player in international student education, institutions had to operate in a cooperative, coordinated way. Rod was amongst the first to identify that educating international students was a rapidly expanding global business that presented a major opportunity for Australia. His role was to assist the Western Australian universities and private colleges to themselves to overseas students, to recruit students and to establish international relationships and agreements with institutions abroad.

In 1989, Rod joined a private college focused on international education.

> I watched what was happening with international students and felt the way they operated could be significantly improved. So I joined an international secondary college and helped to build it out successfully. A few years later it morphed into another college that continues to operate today. That was the beginning.

In the early 1990s, Rod saw a gap at university level that was the opportunity to create what is Navitas today.

> International students were pouring into Australia, and many were failing, particularly at university level. They were basically being thrown into lecture theatres with no support and it was almost a survive-or-die mentality. Students just weren't coping and was nothing to do with their academic ability. It was due to the transitional issues they faced through language, culture, education system and the completely different environment. The failure rates were around 60% of students failing at least one subject in their first semester and something around 30% were failing first year.
>
> I think everybody started to get really uncomfortable with the failure rates and the fact these students and parents were paying good money to come and study here and were going home basically as failures.

In 1994, Rod teamed up with academic Dr Peter Larsen (Fig. 5.2), with whom he had worked in the international secondary college.

> Two guys with an idea around how to deal with the problem of failure for international students sitting around a kitchen table trying to develop a business plan for a single college.

**Fig. 5.2** Dr Peter Larsen and Rod Jones on the day Navitas (previously IBT Education) was listed on the Australian stock exchange, 2004 (Photo courtesy of Rod Jones, Navitas)

Together, the partners approached Edith Cowan University and presented a proposal to set up a pathway program on its campus which would deliver the university's curriculum to 'borderline' international students with extra support and pastoral care during the first year of their degree: smaller classes taught at a slower pace, backed up by English language training and a three-semester yearly calendar. This program aimed to meet the needs and requirements of international students and make a smooth transition into mainstream university by second year.

> It's a half-way house between a disciplinary high school program and the free and easy environment of universities to help these students transition to mainstream universities. We did things like mark the roll because we quickly realised that when people are not turning up, it is not because they are lazy, it's because they are not coping.

The first agreement with Edith Cowan University was sealed later that year, as Perth Institute of Business and Technology (PIBT) (Fig. 5.3). The key to signing this milestone agreement, according to Rod, was trust.

## 5.2 The Entrepreneurial Journey Begins

**Fig. 5.3** Early days—Rod Jones with staff at PIBT Claremont Campus (Photo courtesy of Rod Jones, Navitas)

> I had built a high level of trust with many of the senior university staff over the years and had also built a reputation of success in the area of international education and they were prepared to give me a go. The one thing universities are most conscious of is their reputation and image but I knew the people and they trusted me.
>
> You have to understand the nuances of how universities operate. In dealing with them we have always tried to put in place a relationship that is completely fair and equitable to both sides, where both sides are being fairly rewarded for their contribution. Our university partners trust us, the people in the education industry trust us and government trusts us. I think to have that level of trust is probably one of our greatest achievements, particularly as a private provider.

The pathway college opened at Edith Cowan University's Claremont campus in 1994 with the first student intake in February 1995. The college subsequently moved to the University's Churchlands campus and a few years later to the Joondalup campus.

The college was an instant success, with excellent pass rates and progression rates of about 90% to second-year university.

The pathway program proved to be a win-win situation all around: for parents, who could see the value with the higher pass and progression rates, and because the overall time their children spent studying abroad for a degree was the same; the students, whose education experience in Australia became more positive and successful; and for universities, which had a reliable stream of international students who were better prepared and more likely to succeed, and graduate.

A large part of our success is that we've never compromised on the quality or standards of what we've done, we've always focused on student outcomes and the student experience.

## 5.3  Navitas Grows

By 1997, PIBT had branched out to the eastern states of Australia, setting up programs at Macquarie University in NSW, Deakin University in Victoria and Griffith University in Queensland.

> Getting universities to sign up to this concept, was in part due to timing, but secondly, I had built a reputation as someone who knew what they were doing, and made things happen. . . . They recognised that they had an issue there that had to be dealt with. Universities aren't geared up to deal with the issues faced by international students. And for academics, the last thing they want is a classroom full of people who are not coping. The universities were saying 'If we can find a better way, firstly to reduce the failure rate, secondly, in assisting international students to get where they want to be, and thirdly, to take away some of the issues being faced by their academics then it was going to be a winner. They basically said 'We'll give it a go!'

Gradually, the company continued to expand (Fig. 5.4), with its first international venture commencing in the UK in 2000.

In 2004, PIBT was registered as *IBT Education*, and in 2007, it rebranded and changed its name to *Navitas*. Dr Peter Larsen retired from Navitas in that year but he remained on the Board until 2015 (Fig. 5.5).

Over the years, the company has continued to expand, and now has 31 university pathway colleges across Australia, Britain, the USA, Canada, New Zealand, Singapore and Sri Lanka.

Although the university pathway education model has been copied by other education providers including some universities starting their own 'in-house' programs, Navitas is the largest organisation in the university pathway education space in the world in terms of enrolments.

While the university pathway programs comprise about 70% of its business, Navitas is also the biggest provider of English language colleges in Australia. In addition, it runs a number of industry-focused campuses to train people wanting to work in health services, security and social work.

In 2011, Navitas branched out into media technology training when it purchased the SAE group of colleges for $289 million. There are now 52 SAE colleges offering qualifications, both at undergraduate and postgraduate level in creative media such as gaming, animation, audio and film and television.

With his exceptional knowledge of the international education market, Rod believes that Navitas, like all other Australian and international tertiary institutions, is just as exposed to disruption by technology.

> Education has almost been a little bit immune to some of this disruption but it's coming at us like a tsunami. And you've got to be prepared for it—and certainly we are investing to ensure we are well placed in this space going forward.

**Fig. 5.4** Navitas' success continues (Photo courtesy of Rod Jones, Navitas)

He is also fully aware that the education industry is very vulnerable to regulatory changes.

> The biggest single issue for us is always regulatory risk, in other words changes in government policies. If things do go a little bit awry, their way of solving the issue is normally to smack everybody equally, rather than the ones that have created the problem.

## 5.4 Rod Jones: The Entrepreneur

Rod Jones is a repeat entrepreneur who has risked, lost, risked again and succeeded, numerous times. Over the years he has learnt to take careful, calculated risks.

**Fig. 5.5** The original Board from the Navitas Company listing. L to R: Rod Jones, Harvey Collins, Peter Campbell, James King, Ted Evans, Peter Larsen (Photo courtesy of Rod Jones, Navitas)

> I'm a fairly meticulous person in terms of evaluating and really understanding any opportunity, and I think that this is also what I find when dealing with most people who are successful entrepreneurs. Most of them are pretty systematic and think through the opportunity, and really understand the risk versus the reward equation, and then they take a balanced view about it, is the reward worth the risk, or is the risk too big?

He has outstanding personal initiative, is resilient, is courageous, and has the ability to respond positively to challenges and learn from mistakes.

> My mantra in life is that you cannot change what happens; you can only influence what may happen but you can learn from the past. So many people, when adversity hits, all they do is focus backwards. What could have, should have, may have been done, all that sort of stuff and they spend their time grieving over what has been lost. And for many of them, they just don't come out of it, ever. If they do most become so risk adverse and so concerned about the experience rather than accepting that it's happened. You can't change it. Move on, learn from the experience but focus forward on what might be able to be achieved rather than focusing backwards.

In his late twenties, Rod had been a partner and guarantor for a friend's new and used car franchise. When interest rates dramatically increased, and hit 22% in 1987, the business went into receivership.

> The business went down the tube, and I went down with it. I had to start again at 40. But the one thing I still had was a job.

## 5.4 Rod Jones: The Entrepreneur

> I think a lot of people would have stuck their heads between their legs and disappeared. But one of the strengths I've always had is to focus forward, you can't change what has happened I then started looking for an opportunity which would allow me to bounce back.

Rod's big opportunity came when he identified the need of international students for extra tuition before entering university courses—he provided a solution which he believed could succeed.

> I just saw the problem and recognised there's got to be a better way to do it. If you have a solution, then there's going to be winners. That's the aim of the game always. No point going to people with problems. You go with people who say 'Ok, we've seen the problem. Here's the solution'.
>
> Peter and I basically went seven months trying to reach an agreement with our first university partner without earning a dollar but we had absolute confidence that we could pull it off and get an Agreement signed.

Rod understands the international education market well and knows the statistics. Currently, close to five million international students study around the world; these numbers are expected to grow to eight million by 2025. In Australia, numbers are currently at record high, over half million, with a minimum growth prediction of 4–5% each year. Australia holds 6% of the international education market, behind the USA at 20% and the UK with 9%. The education of international students is Australia's third largest export, after iron ore and coal, worth close to $30 billion.

> The average man in the street would have no idea of the size of the export earnings from international education, and the value-add to the community and to Australia in general.
>
> Parents in developing countries want to give their children a good education but the opportunities in their home country are limited. They save for their children's education from the day they are born.

Rod is a great believer that timing was a big factor in spotting the potential in the education market.

> I think I had seen the opportunity back in 1990 but I also knew that the timing was wrong. At that time, universities had students pouring through their doors. They wouldn't even entertain the thought probably because they couldn't see the consequences of some of the things they were doing and the failure rates of the international students were not really on their radar.

Rod's network was extensive, and at the appropriate time, he called for their support.

> I had an extensive student recruitment network I had built over time, a lot of relationships with high quality agents around the world who I had assisted in getting their businesses established. So when we signed our first Agreement I looked to pull in a few markers 'Guys, I helped you, now it's your chance to help me'.

In 1994, the time was right to launch the first college, *PIBT*.

> It just suddenly went. It was a great idea, the time was right, and when we put it in place, the demand was there to do it. It all fell into place.

In 2004, Rod faced the monumental task of floating Australia's first education company, *IBT Education*, as a public company, with amazing and unexpected results.

> There was no precedent, we were creating it. [...] It was a fascinating day. It was a $1 stock. I still remember sitting there and it hitting $1.60 in the pre-market and thinking 'how good is that!' Suddenly it hit market at listing at $2.20 then went up to $2.90 and settled at about $2.50 at the end of the first day it traded. It was amazing stuff. The day we listed we were worth $800 million.

Rod has encountered numerous highlights, but also some major setbacks.

In 2014, Navitas faced a $38 million loss when Macquarie University, Navitas' biggest client, pulled out of the long-term partnership.

Moreover, issues related to the strong Australian currency, changes to the Australian visa regulation and reputational damage to Australia as a friendly place to study have at various times over the past few years caused a decline in international student numbers, putting pressure on Navitas.

Rod maintains his commitment and optimism, and believes that these issues are always only temporary, from which Navitas can recover.

> Demand for international education is not going to go away. OECD data for the international student market is about 5 million. And they're talking about it to 8 million by 2025. That provides opportunities to keep growing.

Navitas, however, needs to continue to innovate and diversify in order to thrive.

> Students are looking for an education that is worth something and will get them a job and a future. Navitas is about delivering on those expectations.

Rod believes that the future of tertiary education is rapidly changing. This will open exciting new opportunities and new challenges that he is looking forward to.

> In the last 20 years there has been probably more change than in the last 400, and in the last two years the change has been even more rapid—technology is forcing that change to have to speed up more and more. I'm in the school that believes that structure of the degree as it exists today hasn't got a long future.
>
> The world is changing so fast. Who wants to do a four-year degree to find that everything you learnt in the first couple of years, you don't need, or everything you needed to do manually has been replaced by artificial intelligence? I think what we will see are degrees replaced by shorter courses that students undertake and then move out into employment. As change occurs they will then come back to up-skill, re-skill or re-train so we will see people move regularly in and out of the education system.

So what drives this successful entrepreneur?

## 5.5  Recognition for His Achievements

> I love challenges, so to me, the thing that drives me is the next challenge. Sometimes you get caught up in some bad challenges, but most of the time if I had to sit here and do what I did day in, day out, with no additional challenges, then I'd walk away. I'll go find something else to do. I'm passionate in what I want to do and I can't sit still.
>
> I never had a doubt that I could set up a college. Did I ever contemplate what it is today? Never. I had a vision of a college. I never had such a huge vision…

Reflecting back on his life and on his personal achievements, Rod admits that they were never planned—he just took advantage of the opportunities that life offered.

> How you end up, where you end up, who knows? To me life is like a tree, you climb up, you find a branch going in that direction, and that looks interesting, so you head up that branch and you find another branch going off in another direction, so you head up that one, so you end up where you are. If anyone tries to tell me that they can plan your life out, they're living in fairy land. That's the reality.

## 5.5  Recognition for His Achievements

Rod Jones is one of the Australia's most successful and wealthiest entrepreneurs, who has led the successful establishment of the private education sector in Australia (Figs. 5.6 and 5.7) (Navitas News). He is a member of the *Financial Review Rich List*, with an estimated wealth of over $450 million.

Rod has close to 50 years' experience in tertiary education, holding numerous senior administrative positions within government, university and private education sector. He has been instrumental in the development and expansion of the pathway

**Fig. 5.6** Rod Jones addresses international audience, 2013 (Photo courtesy of Rod Jones, Navitas)

**Fig. 5.7** Interview with Rod Jones, 2014 (Photo courtesy of Rod Jones, Navitas)

model across the tertiary education sector in Australia, the UK, Canada, the USA, New Zealand and Singapore (Hiatt, 2016; Navitas News, 2017).

According to Deakin University's Vice-Chancellor, Prof Jane den Hollander:

> Rod Jones is an extraordinary story. Here was an administrator in this far-flung part of the universe. He looked up over the horizon and saw the edge, and just grasped this opportunity. He must be counted as one of Australia's most successful entrepreneurs.
>
> Rod persuaded this quite elitist and disinterested sector to allow those who wanted to, to be able to drink at the education fountain. At the time people were scandalised: 'How dare you make money out of this?' But what he did was give an affordable pathway to those who wouldn't have otherwise had it. Not only are we a better place for it but we are much wealthier. (Durkin, 2017)

In April 2007, Rod received an Honorary Doctor of Education from Edith Cowan University in recognition of his outstanding contribution to increasing student participation in education and the development of the international education sector both in Australia and overseas.

In 2008, Rod was awarded the *Australian Ernst & Young Entrepreneur of the Year* (Figs. 5.8 and 5.9).

In 2010, he was recognised by his colleagues in the Australian tertiary sector with an *International Education Excellence Award* from the *International Education Association of Australia (IEAA)* for his outstanding leadership in international education.

Rod has also established his own family investment office, *Hoperidge Capital*, in Perth, and is a major investor in a number of emerging companies. He is a member of the Business Council of Australia and a fellow of the Australian Institute of

## 5.5 Recognition for His Achievements

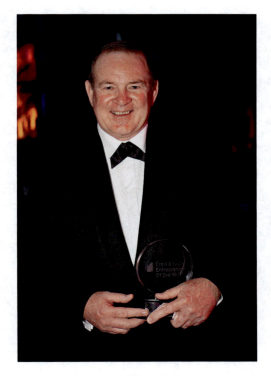

**Fig. 5.8** Rod Jones awarded 2008 Australian Ernst & Young Entrepreneur of the Year (Photo courtesy of Rod Jones, Navitas)

**Fig. 5.9** Rod Jones presented as Australian Entrepreneur of the Year at the E&Y World Entrepreneur of the Year event held in Monaco in 2008 (Photo courtesy of Rod Jones, Navitas)

Company Directors. Rod is also a great supporter of numerous charitable causes in Australia.

Rod stepped down as Chief Executive and Managing Director of the $1.8 billion Navitas in June 2018, and is continuing as a non-executive director of Navitas, of which he remains a major shareholder.

> I'm still going to be around, they don't get rid of me that easily. I'm still the founder, the largest shareholder and the CEO who's built this company to what it is today. I've spent 23 years on a wonderful journey, building this company from two people with an idea, to a company that's spread around the world with 7000-odd staff and 80,000-odd students, and it's very difficult to step completely away from something you love. (The Australian, 2017)

According to media reports, Rod's personal worth is around $370 million. However, it's not money that motivates him, but the sense of personal achievement and accomplishment.

> I've never been focused on dollars, I get more satisfaction out of seeing our students succeed than I do out of making some dollars.
> Knowing where you fit, and the perceptions of people about you, and also getting feedback about issues so that you keep improving—we put a lot of effort into that. We've been successful in a whole range of ways, including financially, but the focus is never on dollars. The dollars are a consequence of doing everything well.

## References

Durkin, P. (2017, September 6). How Rod Jones grew Navitas into an education juggernaut. *The Australian Financial Review*. Accessed September 2, 2018, from http://www.afr.com/brand/boss/how-rod-jones-grew-navitas-into-an-education-juggernaut-20170814-gxvolx

Hiatt, B. (2016, November 15). The WA firm that is educating the world. *The West Australian*. Accessed October 20, 2018, from https://thewest.com.au/news/wa/the-wa-firm-that-is-educating-the-world-ng-ya-120188

Navitas News. (2017, August 3). Navitas Limited (NVT) CEO, Rod Jones. *Executive Series*. Accessed October 20, 2018, from https://www.youtube.com/watch?v=79B_HG57fi0

The Australian. (2017, October 17). Navitas CEO Rod Jones to step back from his pathway colleges. *The Australian Higher Education Supplement*.

# Julie Moss: Photography Studies College (Melbourne)

## 6.1 About Photography Studies College (Melbourne)

Photography Studies College (Melbourne) (known as PSC) is a widely recognised, multi-award-winning tertiary photography college. For over 40 years, PSC has delivered specialised, high-quality and innovative photographic education consistently producing graduates of the highest calibre.

Formally established in 1978, PSC offers a range of part-time and full-time accredited courses ranging from a Certificate IV, Diploma and Advanced Diploma in Photography in vocational education, to a Bachelor of Photography and a Master of Arts, Photography, in higher education. It specialises in commercial, photojournalism and art photography. Lecturers are internationally respected professional photographers, highly qualified, some of the best in the industry, who combine their photographic talent and current practice with their teaching passion—which is greatly appreciated by students of all ages and backgrounds, ranging from school leavers to mature-age students, local and international, all pursuing a profound love for photography.

PSC's dedicated teachers are an important factor in the high quality and innovation of the student experience. The college is consistently rated one of the highest achieving institutions Australia-wide in visual arts as part of the national Quality Indicators for Learning and Teaching (QILT) undertaken by the Australian Government, outperforming all other institutions that offer visual arts courses.

Its students and graduates continue to impact the world of photography with their achievements both locally and abroad. Many of PSC's students have won prestigious awards, have been widely published and have gone on to lead successful careers in all facets of the photographic industry.

Julie Moss is the Managing Director of PSC (Fig. 6.1), with over 30 years' experience in the education and training sector in Australia. She is passionate about photographic education and brings this passion and experience to her leadership of PSC. She is determined to ensure that PSC provides a place where students

© Springer Nature Switzerland AG 2020
L. Hougaz, *Entrepreneurs Creating Educational Innovation*,
https://doi.org/10.1007/978-3-030-28655-2_6

**Fig. 6.1** Julie Moss (Photo courtesy of Julie Moss, PSC)

can learn to see the world anew and be nurtured to develop and achieve their full potential.

Over numerous years, Julie has represented the interests of private education and training providers at the state, national and international levels. She was a founding member of the Australian Council for Private Education and Training (ACPET—the Australian association representing private providers of tertiary education) and served as a Board member and Chair of the ACPET National Board. Julie has been Chair of the National Education Committee of the Australian Institute of Professional Photography (AIPP) and Board member of IHEA (Independent Higher Education Australia)—formerly known as COPHE, Council of Private Higher Education—a peak body representing Australia's high-quality independent higher education providers.

## 6.2 The Entrepreneurial Journey Begins

In 1978, a small photography school with the name of Photography Studies College (Melbourne) was registered in Melbourne by photographer and member of the then Institute of Australian Photography (IAP), the late Roger Hayne.

Recognising the value of education in the photography industry, and the lack of opportunities for photographers to gain formal education at the time, the IAP (now the AIPP—Australian Institute of Professional Photography) gave its formal

## 6.2 The Entrepreneurial Journey Begins

industry recognition to PSC. This esteemed acknowledgement continues to this day with the AIPP.

Roger Hayne was an entrepreneur in his own right. He started his career as a photographer at an early age with a government cadetship. Through his cadetship, he studied photography at RMIT (Royal Melbourne Institute of Technology—now a university), the only photography program offered in the state of Victoria (Australia) at the time.

Amongst his career highlights, he worked as a documentary photographer and filmmaker for the Australian Government's Antarctic Division, photographing and filming scientific expeditions in the Antarctic. He also lectured on photography in the university sector. When he decided to leave the university to establish his own commercial photography business, he taught photography classes to augment his income, initially from his home.

As these grew in popularity, he set up in nearby South Melbourne. A number of photographers became shareholders and teachers, and the college grew from there, until some of their ambitions took hold and they moved to set up a competitor college.

In 1986, Julie Moss met Roger through some mutual colleagues connected to the world of photography.

With a background in sociology and community development, Julie was at the time going through a career transition from a leadership role in community development to a consulting role, undertaking evaluations and reviews of services at local and state government levels.

She had also been involved in the photography sector for quite some time in a number of areas, including documentary and commercial photography, and was considering the more creative career opportunities this sector might offer. She viewed this transition phase as an opportunity to pursue her passion for photography through more formal studies as an adult learner.

Through her photography industry connections, Julie was made aware of some industry and student dissatisfaction with the college's programs. She raised these concerns with Roger and recommended an evaluation of the college's programs be undertaken, along with some focus sessions with students, staff and wider photography industry, which she conducted.

It didn't take her long to uncover the source of dissatisfaction. Key staff in the college, including the then Principal, were in the process of establishing a competitor college, and along with a number of teaching staff, had set in train a program of undermining the college, aimed at taking the students with them to the new 'start-up' college.

Julie recalls that critical time:

> This was a make or break period for the college ... without high energy intervention, it would have closed.

She seized upon the opportunity, took a leading role and convinced those remaining to roll up their sleeves and work decisively.

> It was a particular moment that was serendipitous and synchronistic. I saw an opportunity and took up the challenge. PSC was failing. It was in a parlous state, but I could see its potential amidst its destruction ... I took a risk and worked hard on turning it around.

There was a range of very serious issues, including the conduct of the exiting staff, some of whom were also shareholders of the college. Julie's concern, and her advice to the remaining management and staff, was that if all the energy was to be directed into pursuing some form of legal retribution (which would have been justified), the remaining finances and resources would quickly drain away, and at the end of the day it would not help to gain new students, find new staff or rebuild the college's reputation.

As former Harvard Business School Professor, Howard Stevenson states, entrepreneurship is 'the pursuit of opportunity by an individual beyond the resources under his/her control' (Stevenson, 1984, p.3)... And that is what Julie urged her colleagues to do.

Using her determination and perseverance she contacted every student who had left the college to go to the new opposition 'start-up' college and talked to them about their reasons for leaving. Taking heed of all their feedback, she wished them well and ensured they knew that the door was always open for them to return. The feedback she gained became a crucial resource in guiding the development of a new era for the college.

She tapped into her networks in the photography and community development sectors and rebuilt a completely new team of teachers and support staff.

> Even though it wasn't there at the time, what I saw in the college was the opportunity to create a very unique community of practice centred on photography. Having come from a community development background, I was energised by the possibility of creating an educational environment that was focussed on students and their aspirations, and to bring together people from many different walks of life and age groups to pursue their passion for photography.

However, there were some very real financial challenges to overcome, given the loss of so many students.

> The first year I was at PSC following the split, we only had four students in the final year. It was really touch and go as to whether the college could continue to operate.

Given what had happened, it was difficult to trust any investors, especially if the college was to maintain control and focus on rebuilding its students and its reputation. Julie decided to buy shares into the college.

> To this day I'm not sure how I managed it, but I borrowed money and bought shares in the college. And from there my life took on a new direction!

According to Julie, from that point, Roger never fully regained trust in his business dealings with others, nor with the photography industry. He focused his energies back onto teaching photography, mentoring new teachers and maintaining financial control. He was an inspiring and motivational teacher and ensured that the

## 6.2 The Entrepreneurial Journey Begins

**Fig. 6.2** A PSC staff photo circa 2002. Julie Moss is pictured here second from right (centre row) with the late Roger Hayne next to her (far right) and long-time colleague Jenny Heron to her left. Julie's daughter, Melanie Miller is second from left in front row (Photo courtesy of Julie Moss, PSC)

college's teaching programs were of the highest standard. Julie still meets past students and graduates who acknowledge how much they learnt from him. He once told Julie that he had never wanted to start a college—he had just wanted to be a photographer. Despite the effect of the split of the college on Roger, he was able to put his trust in Julie, and together they formed a new business partnership which eventually became a life partnership until his death in the early 2000s (Fig. 6.2).

As for Julie and her decision to commit to this new venture, her colleagues and friends were not supportive.

> Coming from the community education and arts sector, where everything was publicly funded, they were sceptical of me committing to work in the non-government sector. There was no government support for PSC students. They had to pay full fees if they wanted to learn to be a photographer. This was what was then called a 'commercial' college and not well understood or supported by governments or media for that matter. Sometimes I do wonder what has changed … not much unfortunately …

However, it was here that Julie saw the possibility of creating something new and different. She was energised by that. Her wisdom and management experience gained through her previous small business and community work set a new path for the college and was the catalyst that transformed it into a successful educational and business venture.

## 6.3 PSC Grows

Informed by the feedback gained from her earlier discussions with students who had left the college in the 1986 split and engaging closely with the new students who joined the college, Julie focused on understanding the characteristics and needs of these students, as well as those of the industry. She was determined to ensure that the courses offered in the new era would teach students not only how to be photographers but how to be successful in the photography industry.

> I listened to the students and to the industry and to their views. I learnt how important it was to ensure the college was able to cover the broad spectrum of photography—not just art photography. The feedback was unanimous that the college needed to re-focus and develop strong commercial and photojournalism programs. This is what industry expected and was where the jobs were. So, I tapped into my networks, met with people and gradually brought a new team of people into the college to teach. There was a very strong sense of bringing in new energy, of finding new people who were innovative photographers, had a passion for photography and were great teachers. No easy task. But that was my job. It was crucial to bring in new people with these characteristics.

One of the fundamental features she accentuated was that the people who taught the courses were in and of the industry—this has shaped PSC's culture and has continued to be its asset and characteristic of differentiation to this day.

As this new energy permeated the college, the classes continued to grow. Classes ran day and night—and new Certificate and Diploma programs were made available. Julie's stamina, perseverance and talent ensured that the college would not only survive but thrive.

To do this, she determined that it was vital for the college to gain government registration as soon as that option became available.

> When I first joined PSC, colleges were private entrepreneurial businesses standing outside the government system. In 1991 State governments set about enacting legislation around Australia to enable private colleges to become registered training organisations and to either have their own vocational education and training courses accredited or deliver State accredited programs. I was determined to lead PSC into becoming a registered training organisation and as a result we were one of the first in Victoria.

In 1991, PSC gained Victorian registration as a Vocational Education and Training Provider and gained accreditation for its Diploma of Illustrative Photography course—the first Diploma and the first Visual Arts qualification to be listed on the National Register of Qualifications in Australia. In 1999, its Advanced Diploma of Photography course was accredited.

It took another decade however for PSC to commence taking the exacting steps necessary to become a higher education provider. Some of the reasons for this were due to the hours and years Julie spent focusing her energy and involvement in the growth of a membership organisation that represented private tertiary education and training providers.

> Through my experiences in running the college, it was clear that our sector had very little support from government and that we needed to have our voices heard along with those of government funded providers, industry and in the cases of vocational education and training,

the unions. I was appalled that we had no effective representation and worked with others who were similarly passionate about changing this to ensure our colleges' and our students' voices were heard.

Julie says that the shift to becoming a higher education provider came with doubts and concerns about whether another layer of regulation would dampen the innovative and creative nature of the college's programs. Concerns were raised about losing any last vestiges of autonomy they may have had. In fitting into the myriad governance requirements prescribed into higher education regulation, Julie had lots of questions, none the least of which were:

> Would we risk losing our responsiveness, would it dampen our entrepreneurial and innovative aspirations, our sense of community and, most importantly, our focus on students and their wellbeing and career outcomes?

While it was a long-held aspiration for Julie, she credits its success to the team who drove its establishment, created and led by Julie's now husband Jim Davidson, a former senior Australian bureaucrat with extensive leadership experience in education at both state and federal levels. He agreed to lead the development and implementation of new governance arrangements for PSC as a higher education institution and worked to bring together a talented and highly experienced team of independent Council and Academic Board members all of whom wanted to contribute to creating the next stage of the college (Figs. 6.3, 6.4 and 6.5). In 2011, PSC

**Fig. 6.3** Julie Moss with the PSC Higher Education Council. L to R: Dr Robin Williams, Jim Davidson (Chair), Julie Abramson, John Waters, Phil Ingerson, Dr Laura Hougaz (Photo courtesy of Julie Moss, PSC)

**Fig. 6.4** Julie Moss (centre) with the Academic Procession of the PSC 2018 Graduation and Awards Ceremony. L to R: Sarina Lirosi (Art Major Coordinator), Dr Michael Coyne (Senior Fellow), Neil Stanyer (Course Director VET Programs), Dr Robin Williams (former Academic Board Chair), Jim Davidson (Higher Education Council Chair), Dr Les Horvat (Academic Board Chair), Dr Laura Hougaz (Academic Director), Daniel Boetker-Smith (Higher Education Course Director) (Photo courtesy of Julie Moss, PSC)

gained registration as a higher education institution and accreditation of the Bachelor of Photography course.

Almost a decade on, Julie looks back on the doubts she had and believes it was a crucial decision taken none too soon. In 2017, PSC was accredited to deliver the only Master of Arts Photography course in Australia and is well on the way to its aspiration to be the leading degree awarding photographic institution in the world.

The continued survival of PSC for over 40 years points the way for dedicated photographic education that Australian universities struggle to match. Julie's focus has always been to offer an exceptional educational experience to students of all ages who have a passion for photography—this she has achieved.

Over the years, the college has steadily contributed prominent photographers to the Australian and international scene. PSC has been awarded the photography industry's Australian Tertiary Photography Institution of the Year award for excellence in photographic education for six consecutive years this decade and ranks in the top three of Australia's higher education creative arts institutions for overall education experience (QILT results, 2018 and 2019).

Recent research by the Australian Government Quality (QILT) demonstrates that PSC is one of Australia's leading visual arts education institution.

**Fig. 6.5** Julie Moss at PSC with members of staff and the photography industry

> I am so proud of our talented staff who are all so committed to creating the best experience for our students. Students are rightly very discerning about their education. They know what works for them and what they need in order to have a high-quality educational experience. Our students have spoken and given us the highest possible endorsement.

## 6.4 Julie Moss: The Entrepreneur

In beginning her venture at PSC, Julie would define herself as an 'accidental' entrepreneur. She believes that she was in the right place at the right time.

> I was fascinated by what I found here, I felt this place had the potential to be something unique and special. I'd never really seen anything like it, it was a different form of education and I was drawn to it. And that's really how I came here. What I saw then, and still believe in passionately now,—is that in the college I had the opportunity to knit together my three great loves: community, photography and education, and create an environment in which people of all walks of life can come together, drawn by their own particular love of photography and visual story telling.

She is driven by a desire to make a contribution and make a difference, in addition to using her talents and skills to create something that has worth and benefits to others. The enduring value of education is strongly embedded in her view of the world, as is the need for education to be tailored to suit learners.

> Not everyone is suited to learning in a large institution. Adult learners want flexibility and responsiveness with their learning institution, and they want evidence that the education

environment is closely connected to the industry you are providing the education for. Other types of learners get lost and don't feel they belong in large institutions. People learn in many different ways. With photography we are dealing with a majority of visual or kinaesthetic learners who need to see and experience, rather than listen and write. They need to feel inspired and connected to what they have a passion for. They need that passion to be nurtured and supported.

This is what Julie saw was possible to create in her vision for the college, and it enabled her to activate her skills, talents and values. It aligned with a need she identified amongst aspiring photographers, for a unique photography experience. She understood the market, recognised new opportunities and set in train a direction for the college that aligned with her philosophy and experience.

It's a very strong drive in me. If I can see potential in something and then maybe make a contribution to its development, that's how I express creativity in the world. There was a point at which I realized that my purpose wasn't about being a photographer; I felt strongly that my purpose was about creating an environment in which many people could be photographers, not just me. I am strongly driven that way, I have a strong communitarian value, so being able to make a difference like that keeps me energised.

At PSC we were, and still are, about teaching photography differently, we are about encouraging students to become photographers. We turn students into photographers because this is what we can do and do it well. It is very much our philosophy, and I still hold that value very strongly today ... I strongly believe that anyone can learn to be a photographer, but we as a college have to be able to tap into each and every single person and bring out from them their own visual story and enable them to develop into the best visual communicator they can be.

Julie is highly driven and dynamic, confident and motivated and a high achiever. She feels seriously responsible for the destiny of PSC—as owner of the business she has a strong sense of ownership—and as Managing Director she is in the driver's seat. She is good at managing her strategies to identify and respond to issues that arise and has over time and with experience equipped herself at dealing with the unpredictable, trusting her instinct and having confidence in her decisions. She is aware that her approach needs to be agile and dynamic, and particularly to be collaborative in order to compete in the education sector.

She is also acutely aware of the need to advocate for her sector in order to try to make the conditions more equitable. She continues to be frustrated at the way government policies discriminate against students at private higher education institutions like PSC.

I am strongly driven to work for change in our sector of education to ensure a fair go for our students. The political climate in Australia continues to discriminate against students at private colleges like PSC. I try to find a way to influence those who have the power to make policies to make them see that that they shouldn't unfairly disadvantage us and our students. I can't ever relent on that.

Being a people person is one of Julie's most valuable assets. She is a charismatic figure who relates warmly to everyone.

## 6.4 Julie Moss: The Entrepreneur

She views networking relations as pivotal in supporting her vision and in giving her organisation a voice. She values the photography network, in particular the AIPP, and has always taken an active role on matters related to tertiary education in Australia, serving on boards representing the private tertiary education sector, and on government committees.

In particular, Julie listens to the wants and needs of photography students. From her viewpoint, the customers are right, they know what they want, and by building a positive relationship with them, they remain loyal for life, and support her and her organisation through highs and lows.

Over the years, Julie has gained considerable experience in running a successful business in a challenging environment and has also learnt some good lessons. In particular she has learnt the need to commit fully to an opportunity, to maintain focus on the detail where required and to manage risk by surrounding herself with a team of talented people she trusts, people to assist her in generating new ideas, and in continually redesigning and recreating the organisation to suit the new environment.

She is quick to point out that the college's success isn't all about her (Figs. 6.6 and 6.7).

**Fig. 6.6** Julie Moss with Martin Parr (left), internationally renowned British photographer and member of Magnum Photo Agency, and Daniel Boetker-Smith (right), PSC Higher Education Course Director (Photo courtesy of Julie Moss, PSC)

**Fig. 6.7** Julie Moss with Mr Hitoshi Tajima (UEDA College of Fashion, Osaka, Japan) at the signing of the Memorandum of Understanding (2018). L to R: Mifumi Obata (PSC), Taro Ueda (Ueda Gakuen Educational Corporation), Jim Davidson (PSC), Dr Michael Coyne (PSC), Mr Noda (UEDA) (Photo courtesy of Julie Moss, PSC)

> The college's success today is the culmination of the dedicated and collective input of many talented people who have been prepared to come on the journey and develop a shared vision.

From her beginnings at PSC, Julie has had to steer the college through a range of major challenges and changes, none the least of which has been the rapid technological change to the photography industry over the past two decades.

> The shift from analogue to digital photography has been a major paradigm shift—not only in photography, but also for the college ... and it's far from over. There was no road map for charting the changes we had to make as a college—and the changes just keep on coming. We can never rest!

She sees this as all part of the challenge of running a dynamic enterprise. In 2017, Julie was acknowledged for her over 30 years of outstanding achievements and services to the Australian Photography Industry and Photography Education with the prestigious AIPP Honorary Fellow Award (Fig. 6.8).

Julie continues to be driven in what she does, and wouldn't change it (Fig. 6.9). A few years ago she read an article by *The Guardian* photography critic Sean O'Hagan, who wrote: '*Whatever upheavals it has witnessed, photography has endured. ... Photography, in more ways than one, thrives on a crisis.*' Julie immediately connected to this.

## 6.4 Julie Moss: The Entrepreneur

**Fig. 6.8** Julie Moss receives the prestigious AIPP Honorary Fellow Award in 2017. Pictured here with members of the AIPP Honours Committee. (L to R) Greg Hocking, Richard Bennett and Ian van der Wolde (Photo courtesy of Julie Moss, PSC)

**Fig. 6.9** Julie Moss at PSC (Photo courtesy of Julie Moss, PSC)

Yes! This is not only true of photography, but also of the college. It endures whatever challenges comes its way. I am so proud and humbled by that and by all the special people who have believed in the college and have contributed to our ongoing development and growth. I am so fortunate to be surrounded by the leaders and members of our governing bodies, our amazing staff, our industry supporters, and above all our students and graduates who have all made PSC what it is today.

## References

Photography Studies College. (n.d.). Accessed March 12, 2019, from https://www.psc.edu.au/
Quality Indicators for Learning and Teaching (QILT). (n.d.). Accessed April 10, 2019, from https://www.qilt.edu.au/
Stevenson, H. (1984). A perspective on entrepreneurship. In H. Stevenson, M. Roberts, & H. Grousebeck (Eds.), *New business venture and the entrepreneur* (pp. 3–14). Boston, MA: Harvard Business School.

# 7. Sarina Russo: Sarina Russo Group

## 7.1 About the Sarina Russo Group of Companies

Sarina Russo is the founder of the Sarina Russo Group of Companies, a global leader in education, training and recruitment business with over 1000 employees, originally established in Brisbane, Australia.

The group comprises a range of educational and training programs, employment-related and auxiliary services and close links with large and small employers resulting from long-term consultation and engagement with industry.

*Sarina Russo Institute (SRI)* is a Registered Training Organisation (RTO) educating over 10,000 Australian and international students each year in vocational education and English language courses. SRI delivers industry-focused accredited and non-accredited training, mentoring and job placement services that meets the skilling needs of industry. It also offers traineeships and apprenticeships in Queensland.

- *Russo Business School*, approved as a higher education provider, is the destination for international and Australian students who want to acquire the business skills required to succeed in the globalised world. It focuses on building leaders and gives students the opportunity to continue their studies at university or to enter the workforce. Commencing in 2016 with a Diploma of Business, Russo Business School's strategic aim is to one day become a private university. The programs delivered are focused on the Sarina Russo Group expertise in leadership, entrepreneurship and contemporary management. In partnership with James Cook University Brisbane, since 2006, Russo Higher Education delivers foundation, diploma, undergraduate and postgraduate degree programs to students from 88 countries. Courses include accounting, e-business, business informatics, finance, business administration, information technology, international business, entrepreneurship and tourism.

- *Sarina Russo English*—educates domestic and international students in English language and vocational education. Students can then access university study or vocational training.
- *Joblinx*, a specialised recruitment agency, offers exclusive outplacement student services to provide work experience, internships and part-time and full-time employment opportunities.
- *Sarina Russo Job Access (Australia)* is the largest Australian-owned private sector *jobactive* provider with 93 sites across Queensland, Victoria and New South Wales. This includes Disability Employment Services, one of Australia's largest New Enterprise Incentive Scheme, and agricultural labour placements through Harvest Labour Services.
- *Sarina Russo Job Access (United Kingdom)*, a high-performing employment and training provider established in 2009 that helps long-term unemployed into work through its *Work Program* and *Training Services* that are linked to major employers including Four Seasons, Intercontintental Hotels and ServestGreat Britain.
- *Sarina Russo Apprenticeships*, one of the largest Australian Apprenticeship Centres delivering services in Brisbane, Melbourne, Geelong and Adelaide.
- *Sarina Russo Recruitment* across Australia.
- *Voice Psychologists & Allied Professionals* provides a wide range of assessments, interventions and training programs for people struggling to get back into the workforce. Clinical assessments are also conducted for highly disadvantaged jobseekers.
- *Sarina Russo White House*, a commercial cleaning and facilities management business based on five principles—the right communication, the right supervision structure, the right scheduling, the right staff and the right equipment and materials.
- Sarina Russo Global Initiative (not-for-profit arm).
- Sarina Investments.

*The Sarina Russo Foundation* sponsors and supports activities and events to alleviate disadvantage in local communities through the power of education, employment, health and well-being.

## 7.2 The Entrepreneurial Journey Begins

Sarina Russo is the founder and Managing Director of the Sarina Russo Group (Fig. 7.1). Hers is an inspiring and motivational story of how she used adversity as a stepping stone to massive success.

> The best advice I have ever been given is 'you can do it'. The best advice I can give to anyone is 'if it is to be, it is up to me'. Be passionate and believe in yourself—the rest will fall into place.

## 7.2 The Entrepreneurial Journey Begins

**Fig. 7.1** Sarina Russo (Photo courtesy of Russo Group and BORN Media, Australia)

Born in Castiglione di Sicilia, Italy, one of four children, Sarina migrated to Brisbane with her family from Sicily at the age of five. Her father worked as a handyman on Brisbane's Hornibrook Bridge and her mother at the Golden Circle (food and beverage) factory. They lived frugally, all worked hard, spending weekends at their vineyard, and pooling their money to buy property for the family.

From a young age, Sarina learnt about work, business and making money, and at the age of 10 she was helping her father manage the three apartments and the small vineyard they owned, dealing with the tenants and collecting rent. Sarina holds great respect for her father:

> Everything I am today I owe to the apprenticeship I learned at my father's side. I salute my father for having the guts to leave his tiny village and come to a new country to help us to become more.

With her father standing behind her, 'looking a little bit like a Mafia Don', she interviewed prospective tenants (and often evicted them), negotiated grape prices, even did the family tax returns. 'I was like his apprentice and interpreter... I thought it was the norm' she says, 'Dad taught us that pennies could turn into pounds.' She learnt early that land is a good investment 'I still have every property my father bought. I am a cautious individual, very conservative.'

Sarina's early jobs comprised working as a legal secretary and as a part-time typing teacher. For 8 years straight, Sarina was fired from every job she held as legal secretary. 'I was a typing teacher at night and they fired me there as well,' she said.

She was distressed, eager for work, determined to be independent of her family.

**Fig. 7.2** Early days—Sarina Russo at *The Office Business Academy* in 1979 (Photos courtesy of Sarina Russo Group and BORN Media, Australia)

> They say there are two things in life that you should wish for, desperation or inspiration, and 34 years ago I was truly desperate.

In 1979, Sarina was in urgent need for money, so combined inspiration and desperation, and opened her own small typing school, *The Office Business Academy*, with just nine students (Figs. 7.2, 7.3 and 7.4).

> The fear of failure certainly played on my mind and it certainly motivated me to make sure that I gave it my best shot. I didn't feel optimistic when I started out but I was determined and passionate about being financially independent. I started with a tremendous desire to never work as a secretary again. When I opened the school, I told myself, I'm going to give myself six months and if it doesn't work, I can always go back to a legal job.

After 6 weeks, Sarina knew it was going to work.

> For the first time in my life, I was enjoying freedom and happiness. I made more money in the first three months than I did as a Legal Secretary in a year. I was doing really well.

She soon realised that training was not much use without a job at the end of it, so she promised her students that she would help them find jobs on completion of their course, which she delivered.

Helping others became the key motivator in her life and in her business, and her passion, persistence and self-belief transformed Sarina from a fired legal secretary into an international leader in education, training, recruitment and job creation.

7.2 The Entrepreneurial Journey Begins 87

**Fig. 7.3** Sarina Russo at *The Office Business Academy* in 1979 (Photos courtesy of Sarina Russo Group and BORN Media, Australia)

**Fig. 7.4** Sarina Russo at *The Office Business Academy* in 1979 (Photos courtesy of Sarina Russo Group and BORN Media, Australia)

> I was on fire in every sense. I had set a goal I was going to turn over $1 million—it took me about five years.

In 1988, Sarina expanded her training academy by establishing *The Office International College* offering English Language courses and Study Tour programs to international students in Australia. Her educational and training venture was gradually gaining a reputation nationally and internationally.

## 7.3 The Sarina Russo Group Grows

From her initial successful venture, recognising her own entrepreneurial abilities, Sarina began to exploit a broad range of business opportunities, continuing to build both personal and business momentum and success. Over the years, taking huge risks, she extended into sectors that are compatible with education and training, integrating recruitment and job placement services, workplace training and international education.

In 1994, Sarina's strong personal ambitions drove her to take the biggest risk of her business life, buying a 12-floor high-rise building in the central business district of Brisbane. 'If I don't do this', she argued, 'if I don't follow through and make this building and my business a landmark in the city, I will always regret it. My advice to myself and others is never to regret anything in your life. The pain of discipline weighs ounces, the pain of regret weighs tons' (Russo & Gleeson, 2002, p. 68). In taking this risk, she was fully prepared for the worst consequences, never allowing fear to cloud her judgement. As Gatewood and colleagues point out, 'how entrepreneurs think about themselves and their situation will influence their willingness to persist towards the achievement of their goal.' (Gatewood, Shaver, & Gartner, 1995, p. 373).

Sarina became the first female entrepreneur to privately own a Business City high-rise building. She named the building *The Sarina Russo Centre* and made her office on the top floor. Her new business slogan became '*see you at the top*'. A year later, Sarina established the Russo Institute of Technology Australia to deliver English, business, information technology and hotel and tourism programs.

With a high-rise building to fill, she was fortunate that the government employment agency continued to sign a steady flow of contracts with her to deliver job skills training and job searching, and her business continued to grow. Soon after, fortune smiled on her again. In 1998, the Federal Government privatised the Commonwealth Employment Service (CES), which registered unemployed people to receive welfare payments, and helped them to get into a job. Sarina sensed that this could be a new business opportunity. With her experience, connections and the infrastructure she had created, Sarina won a large Job Network contract to service numerous suburbs of Brisbane and rural areas in the State of Queensland (Fig. 7.5). With this step, she launched into her second major business, which expanded to operate 31 Job Network offices around Australia, under *Sarina Russo Job Access Australia*.

In 2009, Sarina's leadership qualities saw her 'rev-up' instead of closing down when *Sarina Russo Job Access* lost government contracts for 11 of her 19 Queensland offices. Determined to make no one redundant, Sarina reinvented the offices as training centres, expanding into apprenticeship and traineeships

## 7.3 The Sarina Russo Group Grows

**Fig. 7.5** Sarina Russo with Hon Luke Hatsuyker, then Assistant Employment Minister; Hon Scott Emerson, then Queensland Transport Minister; and Hon Peter Beattie, Premier of Queensland (Photo courtesy of Sarina Russo Group and BORN Media, Australia)

through *Sarina Russo Apprenticeships* delivering assistance and advice to apprentices and employers in over 600 industry sectors. By 2015, Sarina had become Australia's largest private employment and apprenticeship provider, with about 40% of her business related to training and 60% to recruitment. She now operates over 200 sites globally in Australia, the UK as well as India, Vietnam and China.

In the meantime, the *Sarina Russo Group* continued to expand and strengthen its vocational and higher education programs. In 2005, Sarina announced the establishment of the *Sarina Russo Schools Australia*, incorporating *Russo English Australia*, *Russo College Australia* (Pathways to University programs), *Russo School of Hotel and Tourism Australia* and *Russo Institute Australia*, cementing its place as a leading English Language and Pathway-to-University provider. This structured and well-planned education and training business focused on customer satisfaction, in addition to profit and growth.

Sarina's dream to run her own university campus came to fruition when Russo Higher Education partnered with James Cook University to open James Cook University Brisbane in 2006, offering bachelor's and master's degrees (Fig. 7.6).

Over the years, Sarina Russo has become associated in the public mind around Australia with education, career training and finding jobs. Her slogan is well known: 'think training, think how to get that job—*think Sarina Russo*'.

**Fig. 7.6** Sarina Russo at launch of James Cook University campus in Brisbane, 2006 (Photo courtesy of Sarina Russo Group and BORN Media, Australia)

## 7.4  Sarina Russo: The Entrepreneur

Sarina Russo is well known for her visionary leadership, her achievements and, in particular, her entrepreneurialism. She has extreme determination to succeed in her business and her life, with huge drive and energy.

> My job is my lifestyle and I love it.

She is profoundly inspired by the power of self-belief, and how it transcends education, training and employment.

> Self-belief creates pathways to opportunities. I believe we all have the potential to make a difference, not from what we hold or where we're from. It comes from what we have in our minds and in our hearts, and it gives us the determination to pursue our goals. Our future begins the moment we set ourselves a goal with these words: I can...I will.

Sarina has the opportunity-driven mindset of an entrepreneur. She strongly believes that vision, change and creation, together with calculated risk-taking, are essential elements for success. Her philosophy is to constantly challenge the status quo, think differently, exceed expectations and deliver with speed and urgency—this, she believes, is why people have trusted her brand for close to 40 years.

## 7.4 Sarina Russo: The Entrepreneur

**Fig. 7.7** Sarina Russo at Harvard University, USA (Photo courtesy of Sarina Russo Group and BORN Media, Australia)

Sarina credits her lifelong love for learning for much of her success. Over the past 20 years, she has been to the US 15 times to attend courses at the Harvard Business School (Fig. 7.7). 'The Harvard Business School for me is a business tool that spurs me to greatness. It's a psychological boost I can't explain' she says. 'When I first went, I was a $10 million business, today the business is worth over $100 million.'

Sarina acknowledges that she could not have achieved her success without support from trusted people in her life. Besides her father, who taught her good business skills from an early age, and her family, she recognises the unwavering support of her brother-in-law, Gerardo Pennisi, who 'has been a pillar of strength and mentor to me throughout my business life. I could never have got where I have without his presence in the business and the wisdom, advice and guidance he has imparted.' She also appreciates the enduring and firm support and encouragement of many of her staff 'because you don't grow a business like ours without the commitment and dedication of talented people who share your vision.'

> I can't believe how lucky I am to have recruited such talented managers who have helped take us to the top in our field. (Russo & Gleeson, 2002, p. 74)

Sarina is particularly grateful to those who have doubted her and have created difficulties and obstacles in her way. 'I say this because the great lesson in my life is that adversity simply means you must regroup, rethink and try again. If your idea is right, your focus is clear and your motives are good, you will succeed' (Russo & Gleeson, 2002, p. ix). She is also grateful 'to all the bosses who fired me, or 'coached me out', though lack of opportunity... I may not have been where I am today had you not, by your actions, strengthened my resolve to find financial independence.' (Russo & Gleeson, 2002, p. xi).

Sarina is not discouraged by pessimists, people who say 'Don't do it ... the economy, the government, the failure rate'. She believes that 'as an entrepreneur, to have more you must become more.'

Her entrepreneurial strategies for success are:

1. Work hard on yourself and your job.
2. Never stop learning.
3. Set yourself short-term and long-term goals.
4. Visualise yourself reaching a goal so clearly that you can taste your success.
5. Persist. Never give up.
6. Above all, believe in yourself and never waver in that belief.

Her future aim is to have a business that continues to be dynamic, still enriching people's lives. Her ambition, however, has changed.

> I have reached a level of contentment, I feel strong, I know who I am, I know my capacity. It's a different level of accomplishment I seek now. It's more about contributing to my community, my country, the world. Now, it's about touching people's lives, being inspiring, having significance.

## 7.5 Recognition for Her Achievements

On the international stage from a young age, Sarina has been recognized as an outstanding visionary, driver and achiever.

In 2002, she was voted, in Paris, as one of the *Leading Women Entrepreneurs of the World*. A year later, she was invited to join the *Women's Leadership Board* of the John F. Kennedy School of Government (Harvard Business School), the Leading Women Entrepreneurs of the World Advisory Board since 2006 and the *Clinton Global Initiative* in 2008 (Fig. 7.8), and is now a member of the *World Presidents Organization (WPO)*. Sarina was also Founding Global Honorary Board member for the *Cherie Blair Foundation for Wome*n.

Sarina is a graduate of the Harvard Business School (USA) Owner/President Management Program and a Global Ambassador for *Same Sky* since 2010, a program aimed at lifting women out of poverty through entrepreneurship.

In Australia, Sarina was the youngest and first female member of the Queensland Chapter of the International *Young Presidents' Organization (YPO)*; she is a member of the state of Queensland Premier's Advisory Board (2000–2012, and 2016–current) and has been the Chairman and Trustee of the *Jupiter's Casino Community*

## 7.5 Recognition for Her Achievements

**Fig. 7.8** Sarina Russo invited to join the US Clinton Global Initiative in 2008 (Photo courtesy of Sarina Russo Group and BORN Media, Australia)

*Benefit Fund* (1995–2013), member of Brisbane's *Lord Mayor's Community Trust* Board (1995–2011), the Council for *Multicultural Australia* Board (2005–2006), Challenger Financial Services Board of Directors (2006–2008) and Queensland Tourism Board (2002–2009), amongst others. Sarina contributes to the Australiana Fund raising funds to acquire and preserve a permanent collection of art works that are Australian by origin or by association.

Sarina was made an Honorary Ambassador for the City of Brisbane in 1996, received the *Centenary Medal* for Distinguished Service to Education in 2001 and has been awarded with the *Multicultural Achievers Award* and the Award—Personal and Other Services Industry category—in 2006.

Sarina is a regular speaker and participant at *Forbes—Asia's POWER Business Women Summit*, and is a *Same Sk*y Global Ambassador, program aimed at lifting women out of poverty through entrepreneurship.

She regularly hosts prominent figures who visit Australia, such as legendary US astronaut Buzz Aldrin, US President Bill Clinton (Fig. 7.9) and former UK Prime Minister Tony Blair (Fig. 7.10).

In recognition of sustained, outstanding entrepreneurial achievement, Ernst & Young recognised Sarina Russo as their "2018 Champion of Entrepreneurship" (Northern Region)—(Ernst & Young Global Limited, 2019). Sarina is a well-known regular expert commentator on education, training and employment for

**Fig. 7.9** Sarina Russo with US President Bill Clinton (Photo courtesy of Sarina Russo Group and BORN Media, Australia)

**Fig. 7.10** Sarina Russo with UK PM Tony Blair (Photo courtesy of Sarina Russo Group and BORN Media, Australia)

international and national media outlets; host of *How to Get that Job*, a television show for over 20 years; and author of her business and motivational book *Meet Me at the Top!*

# References

Ernst & Young Global Limited. (2019). *Meet the 2018 entrepreneurs*. Accessed January 26, 2019, from https://www.ey.com/au/en/about-us/entrepreneurship/entrepreneur-of-the-year/ey-eoy-meet-the-2018-entrepreneurs

Gatewood, E. J., Shaver, K. G., & Gartner, W. B. (1995). A longitudinal study of cognitive factors influencing start-up behaviors and success at venture creation. *Journal of Business Venturing, 10*(5), 371–391.

Russo, S., & Gleeson, B. (2002). *Meet me at the top*. North Melbourne, VIC: Crown Content.

Sarina Russo Group. Accessed May 11, 2018, from https://www.sarinarusso.com/about-sarinarusso/

# Greg Quigley: Jazz Music Institute

## 8.1 About Jazz Music Institute (JMI)

Based in Bowen Hills in Brisbane. Jazz Music Institute (JMI) is a specialist jazz school delivering courses in jazz since 1997. JMI enjoys a reputation throughout Australia as one of the finest jazz institutes in the country, producing graduates with the musical and business skills needed to thrive in the live jazz performance industry. JMI educators are some of Australia's best jazz educators and performers, highly experienced and enthusiastic professional musicians. JMI's faculty staff includes winners of the National Jazz Awards, performers who have extensively toured nationally and internationally, and appeared regularly on television and live shows.

Taught in a jazz context, JMI's accredited courses and casual classes teach concepts behind all styles of music including rock, pop, folk, modern dance music and classical and focuses on improvisation and songwriting.

The institute delivers a Bachelor of Music degree in Jazz Performance which is endorsed by some of the biggest international jazz artists, as well as Certificate III and IV in Music Industry courses for students at secondary school.

In addition to formal courses, JMI offers night-time classes for a better appreciation of jazz in a fun learning environment. JMI's Summer Jazz Clinics have been popular since the late 1970s, delivered in a friendly environment for musicians of all abilities and ages. JMI's Summer Jazz Clinics are also offered in Canberra in collaboration with the Australian National University's School of Music.

According to Wynton Marsalis, internationally acclaimed musician and composer, 'This is one of the first jazz curricula that addresses the entire fundamental range of jazz styles; from New Orleans to Bebop to Modern, it's all there.'

Greg Quigley is CEO at the Jazz Music Institute. He is also a trumpet player, jazz music educator and fervent advocate (Figs. 8.1 and 8.2).

Greg's exceptional achievements include conducting jazz workshops with the Cleveland Symphony Orchestra, during their visit to Sydney in 1973, including orchestra manager David Zauder on trumpet and Al Kofsky on trombone; with US jazz legend trumpet player Don Rader in 1976; and with jazz star Johnny Coles and

**Fig. 8.1** Greg Quigley (Photo courtesy of Jazz Music Institute)

**Fig. 8.2** Greg Quigley, trumpet player (Photo courtesy of Jazz Music Institute)

tenor saxophonist Don Wilkerson and guitarist Jack Wilkins, members of the Ray Charles Orchestra in 1977. From the late 1970s into the 1980s, he toured jazz legends to Australia for concerts and workshops, such as Freddie Hubbard, Woody Shaw, Joe Henderson, John Scofield, Randy Brecker, Mulgrew Miller, Steve Turre, Rufus Reid, Dave Liebman, as well as Terumasa Hino (Japan), Jon Surman, John Taylor (UK) and many more.

In 1981, Greg coordinated the initial Don Banks Memorial Fellowship fund between manager of Pan-Am Airways, John McGee, and the Australia Council. The Fellowship enabled two young jazz musicians, Brent Stanton and David Panichi, to travel to the USA for study and experience.

Greg is an active member of the Australian Council for Private Education and Training and has been member of the ACPET Queensland State Committee for over 15 years (Fig. 8.3).

**Fig. 8.3** Warren Walmsley and Greg Quigley, both members of ACPET State Committee (Queensland) (Photo courtesy of Jazz Music Institute)

## 8.2 The Entrepreneurial Journey Begins

As a late teenager, Greg Quigley developed a great passion for jazz and yearned to learn to play the piano. However, growing up in a small country town where boys were not encouraged to study music, he knew that it just couldn't happen.

> I wasn't good at school, and from day one I had bad experiences at school. I was the ultimate dreamer, and I said 'I'm going to do something one day'. I really couldn't wait to get out of school. School had nothing for me, nothing but horrible experiences. That's when I left home and went to Melbourne.

At the age of 16, Greg went to live and work in Melbourne. There, he would often frequent jazz clubs and gaze for long periods at musical instruments displayed in store windows. Gradually he saved up enough to buy a trumpet, but unable to afford both the trumpet and a case, he brought the trumpet home in a paper bag. His dilemma was that he didn't know how to play it. That was the beginning of his journey with jazz.

Greg took a few lessons from a trumpet teacher, but found that what he wanted to learn was not what the teacher could teach him. So he learnt to play in a brass band, then eventually played in a kicks big band/ jazz big band, but it still wasn't jazz. He also played in a small group, improvising. That was in the 1960s, which was the big trend jazz era, as they called in Melbourne, when one was either a jazzer or a rocker. Greg just loved jazz, and he knew that what he really wanted to play was jazz music.

At the time Greg worked for Rose Music. Australian agent for Yamaha Music, Greg was transferred to Sydney, accompanied by Jeanette, his wife. He looked forward to Sydney, where jazz was more popular: 'I thought: yes, Sydney, it's for me!'

During the 11 years he spent in Sydney, Greg's insatiable passion for jazz, and for understanding how jazz music is learnt, continued to grow.

I was searching, asking 'How do you learn jazz? How do you learn it?' The people who did it just seemed to have a natural ability to hear a song and play it. It was trial and error.

In 1976, the Henry Mancini Orchestra toured Australia, led by the famous American jazz trumpeter Don Rader. Greg contacted him and invited him, at the end of the tour, to join him in Sydney for a series of Jazz Clinics that Greg was planning to organise. To Greg's surprise, Don Rader accepted, so Greg hurriedly advertised the jazz workshops, expecting only trumpet players to attend.

> Well, I got saxophone players, guitar players, piano players, players of all instruments, people I knew who were supposedly top jazz players of Sydney. I was dumbfounded! I said 'What's going on?' I just couldn't believe it.... So that started me on the jazz education path and I decided it was time for a trip to America.

At the time, jazz education in America was still in its infancy—there was an organisation called the National Association of Jazz Educators. In Australia, jazz education did not exist.

Greg had gradually become obsessed with trying to understand how jazz music was learnt and taught. He decided to take a trip to the USA, where he met a number of jazz musicians. One day, by chance, he met Alabama trumpet player Robert McCoy in New York, who played in the Sesame Street Band. Greg recollects how amazed he was to find American musicians so open, direct and sincere in sharing their musical skills and knowledge.

> I recall that we stood on a street corner for over two hours, and all we talked about was trumpet playing and music. I just couldn't believe how much knowledge he had and was willing to share with me. In trying to learn jazz in Australia, it was hard to get knowledge out of jazz players, they were very guarded, and I realised that often they really didn't know. American musicians, jazz musicians in particular, if they can give you any knowledge, they're happy to share it, and they still do today.

One day, reading an American music magazine called *Downbeat*, devoted to jazz and blues, Greg noticed a small advertisement for play-along jazz music albums produced by Jameson 'Jamey' Aebersold, an American jazz saxophonist, educator and publisher. Hoping that play-along albums might be a useful tool to teach beginner jazz playing skills, Greg contacted Jamey, and ordered one. However he was disappointed, as it was aimed at proficient jazz players, unsuitable for beginners. Greg stayed in contact with Jamey, as he highly regarded Jamey's jazz education expertise.

In 1978, the first jazz course started at the Sydney Conservatorium of Music. At the same time, the Australia Council began to award grants to musicians of all backgrounds to travel to New York or America to study. To Greg's disappointment, musicians who were successful would return to Australia, but would not share the knowledge they had gained.

> I thought this was not right. I had a young family at the time, and I could not afford to go to America to study. But I started thinking that if I could get an American to come out here,

then I could get 100 or 200 people who could learn from that person. I figured out that if I charged each participant $20 each, and if I could get 100 people, I would be able to afford the air fare and the accommodation.

So Greg offered Jamey Aebersold a trip to Australia to teach in some jazz clinics that he was planning to organise.

> Jamey kept saying he'd like to come but I could never get a date out of him. So one night I picked up the phone and rang him and I said 'I'm not getting off the phone till you give me a date.' And Jamey said 'No one has ever spoken to me like that, ever.' And I said 'I'm serious, if I've got to sit on the phone for an hour to figure out a date, I'll sit on the phone for an hour. I really want to do this.' So I just bowled him over and I got a date.

In 1978, around Easter time, Jamey arrived, and together with Greg, they ran jazz workshops in Sydney, Melbourne and Adelaide.

> Again, all these musicians turned up. It was incredible!

Gradually an opportunity emerged.

> I started to see that there was a real need for this in Australia similar to those he ran in USA in summer. In talking, Jamey and I came up with the idea of running week long Summer Jazz Clinics, similar to the ones run in America over summer. And Jamey said that he would come to Australia again, and bring with him a rhythm section, guitar, piano, drums, maybe a bass player, and if that worked, then maybe we could bring out this and that. So by the following January, in 1979, 14 Americans walked in through the front door, all waiting for a BBQ to start in Sydney. And that was the start. Of all of these other intermediary things I have done, with the Ray Charles Orchestra guys and various musicians whom I grabbed for the various workshops, this one, this is it!

The idea of week-long highly intensive Jazz Summer Clinics progressively materialised, consisting of a set 5-day program with a practical structure and hands-on playing. Every participant was graded according to their abilities and assigned to an ensemble. This program proved quite hugely successful from the beginning; however, it was very costly, and after 4 years it became very expensive.

Regrettably, at the same time, Jeanette's health deteriorated. Facing these pressures, a teaching position came to Greg's attention with the Queensland Education Department, which was then hiring professional musicians to develop instrumental music programs in secondary schools, as the Training Colleges and Universities were not able to fill this gap. Greg was hired, and moved from Sydney to Brisbane with his family. For over 15 years, he taught and built a successful music program in a reputable secondary school, gaining sound teaching expertise. During the school holidays, he continued to organise week-long jazz clinics in Sydney, Melbourne, Brisbane and Townsville.

> I just couldn't let it go, and I still had that passion for jazz.

**Fig. 8.4** Early days of *Jazzworx!* Greg Quigley with Jeff Jarvis, President of Kendor Music Publishing, USA, also distributors of JMI jazz education play-along series (Photo courtesy of Jazz Music Institute)

When the Queensland Education Department decided to transfer him to another school only 2 years prior to his retirement, Greg resigned from teaching. After some serious consideration, in view of his passion for jazz music, and with the teaching expertise he had gained over the years, Greg opened a small jazz music CD store in Paddington in Brisbane, with his daughter Paula and son Daniel. Greg began to teach jazz and music classes in the evenings as well as week-long jazz courses, basing the teaching program on past clinics he had offered around Australia. This business, known as *Jazzworx* (Fig. 8.4), focused on improvisation of jazz music for beginners, which, as he had personally learnt, was not taught in other music courses. It was a gap that he could fill (Fig. 8.5a, b).

> They couldn't cater for beginners who wanted to know 'How do I start to improvise?' They didn't say 'Well, you've learnt a scale, so the knowledge has to be there, and now you add rhythm'. These are the things I started discovering. So with pianist Vince Genova, I developed a method of our own, and I persevered, and one day I said 'God, We have written a curriculum. Look at this, it's a complete curriculum: it starts at the beginning and it goes all the way through to the advanced stage. We've got to look into this!'

## 8.3 JMI Grows

Having developed a jazz education curriculum, Greg began to enquire about formal vocational education and training. He submitted the teaching program for approval, and in 1997 it was accredited as an Advanced Diploma of Music, and his teaching institute was approved the same year as a Registered Training Organisation (RTO) with the new name of *Jazz Music Institute*.

The first cohort of Advanced Diploma students graduated in 1998 (Fig. 8.6). Enrolments grew, and business expanded.

## 8.3 JMI Grows

**Fig. 8.5** (**a**, **b**) Article featuring Greg Quigley, in *The Australasian Contemporary* Jazz Music Magazine, September/October, 1981 (Photo courtesy of Jazz Music Institute)

at this level but it can be quite instrumental in planting the seeds for bad habits and feelings which can and usually do carry over into later years and will be less than beneficial toward a successful career in music. I see an incredible amount of trivial things like this that have completely wrecked good bands, destroyed friendships, and ended up with the loss of jobs for the musicians involved. *It takes a terrific drive to learn and win to make it in this business, but more importantly, it takes a high sense of ethical and moral obligation. You'll never make it in the long run by cutting your brother's throat to get a job.* Somewhere underneath all of the "games", music is a thing of great beauty and joy and this awareness is the determining factor in the kids future success and happiness through his or her involvement in music.

Personal involvement is a huge but vital subject in itself. I have seen large numbers of kids coming out of high schools & colleges that play well, it has sent me back to "the woodshed" in some cases. But through closer observation I have noticed that most are incredible instrumentalists technically, yet have very rarely enough, if any, roots established not only jazz-wise, but classically as well. The majority of the young trumpet players are struggling like crazy to play a double C, yet never sat down and listened closely to the likes of Clifford Brown, Charlie Parker, Kenny Dorham, and even more distressing, to Louis Armstrong. Sure, it's an asset to be able to play in the high register, but you can't make a decent living doing *ONLY* that and it's for sure that a high note doesn't qualify you as being a good or great musician.

With my private students and those at clinics (time permitting), I spend the majority of time working to make them more aware of the aesthetic or creative values of music. I do this generally by concentrating on how to listen to music through getting your mind "in tune" or interlocked with that of the players on the record and freeing your mind of methodical analysis at first then letting the music take you on a "journey" with the players. By doing this, the kids get involved with the music experience in a more creative rather than analytic sense. It is a very valuable technique to analyze scales and chords, but the prerequisite should logically be the personal involvement. I strongly favour the use of earphones when available for listening as it helps to eliminate outside distractions which interrupt the "trip". Even closed eyes has been extremely successful to heighten sensitivity. Nearly always, I can see and feel a student "come alive" to the emotional feelings of jazz and can sense his degree of understanding rise to great heights in a short span of time.

I jockey back and forth between structural analysis and aesthetics as both are vital. There are currently many improvisation methods available on the market the majority of which have made jazz so technical and scientific that the students of same essentially becomes a mathematical computer with limited or no sensitivity. *The methods that I generally advocate (second to just doing a lot of playing with guys better than you) are the ones that contain a play-along record with a good rhythm section as the practical experience a student gets from actually playing far exceeds that of the written text.* Let it also be said that this involvement does wonders for a good unity in playing ensembles and even more importantly, it lays the foundation for a more secure and confident attitude towards being a good soloist and a good "musician".

This brings me to the real "capper" . . . CONFIDENCE. What is it and how do you get some for yourself and for your students? I'm sure we all have at one time or another felt those "butterflies" dancing just below the rib cage and remember well how adversely it affected our ability to think, play, and communicate. In this business it's commonplace to experience this even for a great many of the seasoned pros. But a real pro will do a good job of hiding the panic from his fellow musicians and the leader and more often will have developed a "system" of handling or eliminating it. A musician will also do his best when relaxed even though he may be playing with a great deal of energy and excitement. The relaxation must be there. Probably the most common source of this lack of confidence is self-doubt and/or invalidation and next to that is allowing yourself to be overly influenced by other people's evaluations of you and your abilities.

Many students feel they must compare themselves to the old pros and also feel a strong desire to prove themselves or impress their fellow players. Some of these are valuable but all things must have a balance. *The kids ought to compare themselves to the pros for the learning experience and awareness, but the "pro" should never take precedence over the student's own reality and feelings.* He must pursue his own point of view and realize that everyone else is hopefully doing the same thing. Again with my students, I work very hard to help the kids realize if, when, and how they subtly wipe themselves out. It really opens up the doors for them as far as maturing and gaining self-confidence. The key here is to stop finding so many faults with your playing while still realizing your current limits and exactly what you must do to improve.

A little cockiness is far better a choice than apathy. Given sufficient rein to mature, the obnoxious and destructive qualities of over-confidence as related to the real ability, will dissipate and you'll find yourself with students who are highly able, talented, and enthusiastic about their music. It is through greater understanding of music that confidence comes up. Areas that are, for the most part, a mystery to the youngster will quite obviously hamper his attitude about his ability.

Another important area of attack is one of eliminating the "seriousness" that robs us of the enjoyment of life and music. I do feel that sincerity, devotion, and persistent hard work with eyes and ears wide open will bring about much more success than the laborious "seriousness" that we are often taught in our early years. In its place, we develop confidence not only in ourselves, but I think we all ought to help each other with this. I also feel that real participation in music should bring about lots of happy, smiling faces and when I see the opposite, I begin to wonder whether or not the kids are getting the best we can give. *TALENT IS A LACK OF BARRIERS*; let's help each other knock them down.

JAZZ MAGAZINE IS PROUD TO BE ASSOCIATED WITH THE

AUSTRALIAN JAZZ FOUNDATION

SUMMER JAZZ CLINICS:
SYDNEY: *January 18–24, 1982*
MELBOURNE: *January 25–31, 1982*
(Enquiries (02) 712 7383)

**Fig. 8.5** (continued)

## 8.3 JMI Grows

**Fig. 8.6** First graduation of JMI's Advanced Diploma students in 1998 (Photo courtesy of Jazz Music Institute)

> We were delivering the course part time, then four full time students enrolled, and every year, it grew and grew and grew. We moved seven times in a 15 year period as we outgrew the premises.

Greg soon realised that the best and most enthusiastic students completing the Advanced Diploma at JMI would often continue to study a Bachelor of Music degree at the Queensland Conservatorium of Music. There was obviously a strong demand for a degree course in jazz music.

> We applied to the Office of Higher Education to become a private higher education provider delivering a Bachelor of Music in Jazz Performance. With two attempts and 4.5 years later we were finally approved.

Greg had been involved in the development of the jazz degree course at the Queensland Conservatorium of Music, from its beginning right to its completion, and then its review.

> I had kept an eye on it over the years, and I used to shake my head as I didn't agree with it, with the quality of teaching and the quality of the curriculum, and I would say 'I can do better than that'. With all of what the changes I had made in my life, I decided to do it.

In 2010, JMI was accredited to offer the Bachelor of Music in Jazz Performance (Fig. 8.7).

Amid all of the work, the teaching, the clinics, the ventures, Greg kept playing and loving jazz. He recognises Jeanette's important role in keeping the family

**Fig. 8.7** Greg Quigley and the Bachelor of Music in Jazz Performance graduates at the inaugural graduation ceremony held at JMI's campus' *Turnaround Jazz Club* in 2011. (Photo courtesy of Jazz Music Institute)

together, supporting the business and encouraging Greg to continue playing jazz over the years.

> Without the support of my wife it would never have happened, and I couldn't have survived. She had been there through all of it, and picked up all the pieces, and did the administration and whatever had to be done. And one day she looked at me, she shook her head and said 'Why did you do it?' She had never stopped to look at it until then.

Greg is the inspiration behind JMI's success. His motivation for all he has done and achieved stems exclusively from his relentless passion for jazz and his insatiable hunger to learn more about jazz music and jazz improvisation.

> It was passion and it's still there. I'm still passionate about jazz music, it's reverence to the style of music, to the roots of music.

He had always wanted to learn more and more, and along the way, he has given other learners knowledge and opportunities that he had dreamt about having since his youth.

> Really, I had wanted to do it for me, it kept driving me. It's amazing what I learnt along the way because I was so mixed up in it, in all those jazz clinics, and in bringing all those guys out from the US, that motivation to drive the whole education vehicle. And I just wanted to do it for me, for my playing. The reason was that I wanted to be a really good jazz musician, it's not for the money, it's for the music, and it still is. We wouldn't be doing what we're now doing without my passion for jazz.

## 8.3 JMI Grows

Greg believes that his unwavering passion for jazz music is behind the success of JMI and that it must remain a priority for his children and the institute.

> First thing is the music. I say to my sons and daughter that the music is paramount, concentrate on quality. The income will come. With the music, and we teach at a high level, the income will come. And it has.

JMI is a unique music institute, and it is now a successful family business. With three out of four of Greg and Jeanette's children in the business (Jeanette sadly passed away in 2012), JMI is now in the skilled hands of the second generation: Nicholas Quigley is Chief Executive Officer, Daniel Quigley is Head of School as well as an accomplished jazz trumpeter and teacher, Paula Girvan is Registrar and Course Coordinator and Greg continues to support the institute from behind the scenes.

JMI's successful teaching program is highly recognised by jazz experts around the world.

> Our course has been endorsed by a number of experts, including Wynton Marsalis[1] who is the "god of jazz" and multi Grammy Award winning jazz trumpet player. My son Dan met him in December 2012 to ask his opinion and advice about our course structure. Wynton was astounded and has subsequently endorsed the course. It is the only jazz course ever endorsed by him.

This led to a partnership with Jazz at Lincoln Center, where Wynton Marsalis is CEO, to deliver in Australia their 'Essentially Ellington' program for high school student. The Jazz at Lincoln Center's mission is 'to entertain, enrich and expand a global community for jazz through performance, education, and advocacy.'

> From our first downbeat as a summer concert series at Lincoln Center in 1987, to the fully orchestrated achievement of opening the world's first venue designed specifically for jazz in 2004, we have celebrated this music and these landmarks with an ever-growing audience of jazz fans from around the world. (https://www.jazz.org/history/)

JMI and Jazz at Lincoln Center continue as partners in presenting the *Essentially Ellington* Down Under Regional Festival. In 2018, the festival was held in Brisbane, Perth, Adelaide, Melbourne and Sydney, offering high school jazz bands and music directors/musicians of all sorts some excellent performance and professional development opportunities.

JMI competes with the best university courses in Australia, in particular Sydney University and WAAPA (Western Australian Academy of Performing Arts) at Edith Cowan University. It puts great effort and finances into maintaining its high reputation.

---

[1] Wynton Marsalis is a famous trumpeter, composer, teacher, music educator and artistic director of Jazz at the Lincoln Center in New York City, USA.

We aim to be on a par with Sydney University and WAAPA. That's our determination. We know from outside people coming in and making observations that we're on par with them.
[...] We don't compromise on quality and we support two of our teaching staff to fly from Sydney every week. We want a high standard and we put the demand on ourselves, and it comes out in the students. It's only a couple of weeks back when we had two ensembles play in our jazz club at the Institute on a Thursday night, it was a combination of undergraduates and graduates. I just listened and shook my head: boy, it is paying off. It was such a high level. Really, really high level! They could have held their heads up anywhere in the world, the playing is superb. We're getting such a great reputation. Our students go out and play and everyone is amazed that they can play. They're really good musicians. We're tough but we care for and nurture our students. We are known for our family approach. To learn to play jazz requires a high level of discipline. We're really hard on our students but we're getting the end result of high quality performers.

Greg is naturally proud of his achievement of establishing a reputable tertiary educational institution that specialises in jazz music (Figs. 8.8, 8.9 and 8.10).

Having a passion for music and having a passion for education, for people to learn, and to hear people improve, is so rewarding. I feel we have done something really good for our students. I'm not religious in any way but I firmly believe that we're on this Earth to do something, and I've learnt that from all this and I've gotten so much from out of it, that each step I've moved along, I've become more determined that I was going to achieve something. I guess that's the rewarding feeling of seeing someone grow. It's fantastic!

**Fig. 8.8** Greg Quigley (centre front) with the Quigley Power Brewing Rock (Photo courtesy of Jazz Music Institute)

## 8.3 JMI Grows

**Fig. 8.9** The Quigley Moorhead Big Band (Photo courtesy of Jazz Music Institute)

**Fig. 8.10** Greg (centre front) with the Quigley Big Band (Photo courtesy of Jazz Music Institute)

## 8.4 Greg Quigley: The Entrepreneur

Greg's obsession for jazz music and his admiration for great jazz players have always been his driving force.

> I didn't like school, but then, when I started music, I had no trouble practising every day, and I wanted to do that, I really wanted to play. I used to go to jazz concerts now and again, and there would be big name players that had come from the States and other musicians. I got so inspired, and I'd think 'I'm going to go home to practise'. I didn't get discouraged by hearing brilliant players. I was fascinated by them, and they were brilliant because they worked at it. They didn't tell you 'Oh, I'm just naturally brilliant' None of them were. There was talent but they practised and worked at it for long hours.

Greg's love for jazz and his struggle to learn how to improvise and to obtain knowledge from Australian jazz players, together with his lengthy teaching experience, made it possible for him to identify a gap in jazz music education, in particular for beginners. He was confident that he had the unique combination of knowledge, skills and creativity to develop his idea into an educational business—it was an opportunity, he set a goal and aimed to achieve it.

Entrepreneurs are creative, they enjoy what they do, their venture is a challenge they can't or won't pass on.

> There was something I've always had in me, and I used to always think 'There's got to be a better way to do this.' And the more I learnt and persevered, I found, yes, that there is a better way.

For Greg, his venture was a natural step.

> It never frightened me. It was almost like I had to do this. I had gone too far.

Like other entrepreneurs, Greg is not motivated by money. He has always had a strong yearning to learn more about jazz and share the knowledge with others.

> The passion meant that I wanted to do it for myself, but what I got out of it was that I used to watch people come in when we were doing those week long clinics, and they could play their instruments, but at the end of the week, you would just go 'Wow!' It was astounding, the transformation in one week. We had good educators, very encouraging people, and a good attitude. This would drive me to do more.

Jazz music has driven his motivation beyond boundaries, keeping him focused and determined.

> I was determined that I was going to achieve something. Total perseverance. It was the music that was so powerful and so it just kept me going.

Greg is energetic and hard-working. Despite his achievements, he admits that it has often been tough and stressful. The pressure is often difficult to cope with.

## 8.4 Greg Quigley: The Entrepreneur

**Fig. 8.11** Greg Quigley at Jazz Music Institute in Brisbane, 2017 (Photo courtesy of Jazz Music Institute)

Totally hard work. Don't give up. [...] I can remember times when it was financially tough. And yes, you do have those moments of despair, and a few wines, and you think 'Oh God, how am I going to get out of this one?'

Greg manages risk by surrounding himself with trusted people.

I've got some great friends in Sydney in the music scene who've remained really good and trusted friends all that time.

His family members, who are now part of the JMI family business, are his trusted team and partners—they share the decisions and, more importantly, the risks.

Each of them has their qualities, each has a role, and the whole thing is in very good hands.

Greg has built many networks in Australia, and in particular in the USA, over the past 20 years, people who know, admire and appreciate his obsession for jazz and his outstanding accomplishments.

One night, a jazz saxophone player called Sandy Evans was playing at one of our campus Thursday night concerts. Just before she played the last song, she announced 'I want to say something before I finish. I wouldn't be standing here tonight if it weren't for Greg Quigley. Greg affected hundreds of us, not just a few. We all still talk about what he did. And he's still doing it!'

All these attributes have helped Greg to become the jazz music entrepreneur he is today (Fig. 8.11).

## References

Jazz at Lincoln Center. (n.d.). Accessed March 20, 2019, from https://www.jazz.org/
Jazz Music Institute. (n.d.). Accessed March 23, 2019, from http://www.jazz.qld.edu.au/

# Leanne Whitehouse: Whitehouse Institute of Design, Australia

## 9.1 About Whitehouse Institute of Design

Whitehouse Institute of Design is one of Australia's leading design training institutions offering an extensive range of higher education, vocational education and non-accredited short courses in fashion, interior design and creative direction and styling.

Leanne Whitehouse, the Founder and Managing Director of the Whitehouse Institute, is well known in the industry and highly respected for delivering high-quality education. Through her institute, she has guided a generation of impressive Australian fashion designers, including Akira Isogawa; Alex Perry; Lisa Ho; Sharlene Flemming, head designer of Vivienne Westwood's *Anglomania*; and Camilla Freeman, topper of *Camilla and Marc*.

The Whitehouse School was founded in Sydney in 1988 by Leanne Whitehouse, offering short unaccredited courses in fashion. In 1992, the first accredited courses in fashion at Diploma and Advanced Diploma were offered.

Working in the area of design, it soon became obvious that international partnerships were pivotal to the institute's success. In 1994, the Whitehouse School commenced a long-standing international relationship with the Accademia Italiana in Florence, Italy, a renowned private design school specialising in fashion, costume design and interior design.

Soon after, in 1996, Whitehouse offered the first accredited courses in interior design, spanning from architectural drafting, construction and materials knowledge to the formation of conceptually based design ideas, aiming to meet the needs of commercial, residential or corporate clients.

In 1999, new courses in creative direction and styling followed, with a multidisciplinary approach from across various visual creative industries, combining design and implementation of creative strategies for fashion, beauty, publication design, interior spaces, visual merchandising, food and lifestyle, campaign creation and events management.

In early 2004, the Whitehouse School was renamed and became the Whitehouse Institute of Design.

In 2008, Whitehouse Institute opened a new campus in the Historic Royal Mail Exchange Building of the Melbourne Central Business District and expanded its teaching program into higher education, offering a Bachelor of Design in both Sydney and Melbourne.

The Melbourne Campus is a state-of-the-art, purpose-built campus covering 6000 m$^2$ of design environment in the heart of the city. Many fashion designers show their collections there while companies such as Gerber Technology run industry training days in-house, and Myer has launched seasonal collections to the media and guests on the top floor.

In 2008, the beautiful Melbourne campus hosted Australia's first fashion reality TV show, *Project Runway, Australia*, an elimination-style series that appealed to fashionistas of all ages, with over 1.5 million viewers. The show continued to be filmed at the campus for several seasons, and its popularity has helped to promote the Australian fashion scene and sales across the country.

In 2010, the Whitehouse Institute in Sydney relocated to a new campus in the city's popular design precincts of Saint Margaret Square, Surrey Hills, in HPM's former electrical parts manufacturing factory, boasting expansive spaces and views of Sydney Harbour (Fig. 9.1).

In 2012, Whitehouse began to offer new higher education qualifications: the Bachelor of Design (with specialist streams in fashion design, interior design and creative direction and styling) and a Master of Design. The Master of Design program balances design research with interdisciplinary studio practice, promoting a socially responsible and sustainable, professional and innovative culture that promotes lifelong learning for the betterment of the community.

In 2013, Whitehouse celebrated 25 years in Design Education by holding exhibitions and fashion runways at both campuses titled *A Night in White*.

Due to the critical shortage of teachers in design and technology, Whitehouse Institute has partnered with Southern Cross University (SCU) to offer students the opportunity to combine recognised industry training and their creative skills with a teaching qualification in design and professional teacher qualification in innovation and technology education, ensuring graduates have flexible career opportunities. SCU was selected for this joint venture because of its regional base and its high-quality Bachelor of Technology Education degree, one of the very few in the market with a focus on innovation education.

Since 1990 Whitehouse has implemented a four-block program for Year 11 and Year 12 High School students that contributes to their final high school results which, along with short High School Workshops, currently teaches more than a thousand students annually throughout Australia.

The NSW government has also engaged Whitehouse to deliver retraining courses for high school teachers to train as textile and design teachers, and teachers are awarded graduate certificates in higher education.

Along with fashion design and creative direction and styling, Whitehouse Institute continues striving to provide the best interior design education and practice. It

**Fig. 9.1** Whitehouse Institute's campus in Sydney, Australia (Photo courtesy of Whitehouse Institute)

has produced some of Australia's leading designers. Amongst the graduates of Whitehouse Institute are Tamara Ralph of couture label Ralph & Russo; Georgie Williamson, a major designer for Echo in Los Angeles; Rehanah Bouchan, head accessories designer for Gucci, Switzerland; and Lucy Rickard, designer for the Webster Group (David Lawrence).

## 9.2 The Entrepreneurial Journey Begins

Born in Perth, Western Australia, Leanne Whitehouse (Fig. 9.2) knew from the age of four or five that she wanted to be a designer (Casamento, 2012).

> I had a calling and I spent my childhood making Barbie doll dresses and drawing pictures of clothes. Barbie was absolutely my inspiration. I would go to school with all the Barbie clothes I'd designed and sewn. But I preferred drawing.

**Fig. 9.2** Leanne Whitehouse (Photo courtesy of Whitehouse Institute)

After living in Perth, then Melbourne, Leanne moved to Sydney in her early teens with her family and twin sister, where she found the change in schooling systems challenging, never really settling well into formal secondary education. With her mindset on wanting to be a fashion designer, she left school at the age of 16 and was accepted to study design at the National Art School, located in the historic Darlinghurst Gaol site in East Sydney. As an impressionable 16-year-old who lived in the conservative outer suburbs, she was overwhelmed by the colourful lifestyle and people in the area. She was the youngest student in the class, struggled through her first year, topped the class in second year and third years and was presented with the first Fashion Group Scholarship. At the end of her course, aged 19, Leanne was invited to teach part-time evening classes at the National Art School, in addition to her full-time day fashion designer job.

> I always had two or three jobs going at the same time, which is great because you keep alive as a designer.

She worked as a designer for well-known fashion brands such as Daily Planet, Carla Zampatti and Dorelle of Sydney. Soon after, she began to teach full-time, as well as designing part-time, and at the age of 28 was appointed Acting Head of the Art School. 'I realised then that that's where I was always meant to be, I found my home there.' she says.

Then suddenly, one day she was 'hit by a bolt of lightning', craving to expand her horizons and experience the world. She sold her belongings and went to New York to live for a few years, working in the fashion industry for up to 100 hours a week,

## 9.2 The Entrepreneurial Journey Begins

then went off to Jamaica, where she led a fun life, becoming windsurfing champion in 1984.

She returned to Sydney, found part-time employment teaching fashion at a TAFE institute (Technical and Further Education—government-funded vocational tertiary education), met her partner and had her daughter, Billie. That's when things got tough.

> I had decided to leave Billie's father when she was one, and I remember thinking 'How do I take a child out of all of this?' There was no choice—my day care cost $450 a week more than what my take-home pay from TAFE. I was worried, thinking 'How am I going to take care of day care and rent and food?'

With a young baby, a breakdown in her relationship and A$1300 in her bank account, balancing family and personal requirements and responsibilities was overwhelming, but Leanne had aspirations that motivated her to search for new opportunities.

> My colleagues from TAFE and I had all discussed starting a private design school, and we knew that there was great need for it. Once I had my baby, I realised that children are very expensive, and TAFE was not going to pay the rent. I realised very quickly that I needed to start a business. That's the bulldozer energy you get when you have to provide for a child!

Driven by the need for improvement in her life, she relied on her knowledge and experience in the fashion industry and decided to start her own private fashion design school with a new industry-focused approach to design education.

> I thought 'Well, I've talked about it for a long time, I certainly know a lot about teaching, and teaching design, and now is the time to go and do it . . .'.

She knew the market well and knew there was a need for it.

> I had lengthy experience in teaching designers, and at the National Art School we would turn away 1000 students a year as we couldn't fit them in. So I thought, 'I've got this opportunity, and I'll write the syllabus and curriculum'.

Building on her experience and expertise, Leanne felt confident that she could sustain a new fashion design venture. Using the little money she had in the bank, she felt ready to take a risk—after all she had nothing to lose. So she placed an advertisement in a popular Australian women's magazine, offering courses in fashion design at a new school, the Whitehouse School.

> I put one ad in *Cleo* and I received 25 phone calls, and 24 people gave me their money. I remember interviewing all these kids with Billie bouncing on my lap in my small rented cottage. I had no premises but all these people gave me their money, which was extraordinary, but then I had to race out and find premises, which I found in the city. I knew nothing about business, absolutely nothing. I didn't have any furniture. I went to an auction and bought all the furniture and sewing machines for the school. . . . That was in 1988.

She recalls those difficult early days, working hard, struggling to make the business survive, which it did, with Leanne's intense commitment, discipline and determination.

> People said to me it takes five years to get a business off the ground, but for me it was seven years and seven days a week, and of those seven days a week I would never consider taking a day off because you just couldn't, there was too much work to do, and I couldn't afford to pay anyone else to do it.

Supported by her mother who helped to look after young Billie, Leanne worked relentlessly, striving to achieve her goals.

> Billy was born in 1987, she was one year old when I started the school, and she grew up at the school. Thankfully I had my Mum to help out. I never saw Billie, only when I went to bed at night. It was a great cost... but it had to be that way.

Having no financial experience, funding the new venture proved to be problematic. Obtaining a bank loan was impossible; however as Leanne acknowledges, she was particularly lucky.

> For the first six months it was self-funding from the deposits the students paid, and then we ran out of money. Then two extraordinary events happened. A teacher from Prairiewood High School called me and asked me to give a two day workshop on how to draw and how to design, and each day was paid $50, so that kept us going a little bit further. Then when we ran out of money again, my best friend, John Henry, mortgaged his house, gave me the money and told me to pay him back when I could. He gave me $50,000 which saw me through into the next year [...] Thank goodness that from that year, the students increased every single year and I paid John Henry back in February of the next year. And we've never borrowed any money since.

As Leanne soon discovered, being a private education provider and competing with government-funded TAFE was, and continues to be, quite challenging.

> It was hard, as we had to provide much more than a TAFE would, because the students were paying for it. We had to be much better, give a lot more, and care a lot more, and be more focused and determined that our students were going to be successful and better than any other school in Australia.

Through advertising and word of mouth, enrolments gradually increased, and over the years the school expanded.

> We've had a wonderful journey of self-funding and learning as you go... Gradually we went from one little room in a basement in Liverpool Street in the city (of Sydney), to taking over most of the building, and having outgrown that building, we moved to our beautiful premises in Surrey Hills.

## 9.3 Whitehouse Institute Grows

Over the past 30 years, both Leanne Whitehouse and her Institute have adapted, innovated and survived many changes in both the fashion industry and education.

> In my mind's eye I didn't have a picture of what it would be like, but now I have a picture it could be a lot bigger, business is exciting and design education is exciting, and education in Australia is exciting.

Leanne believes that fashion design is a hands-on experience, and that's what she is committed to giving to her students:

> While technology has changed, one still has to have skills in being an illustrator, or making the model, or taking the photo, or making the garment, and I believe my students will be the most sought after on the planet because design is not theoretical, it is a process—and so much learning comes through this process. At TAFE it was all about cutting down the number of student contact hours and making the course theoretical, which does not make you a designer. The world is waking up, you can't be a theoretical designer, you can't just talk about it, you actually have to be able to do it.

Leanne's professional background as an expert fashion designer has been essential to the success of her institute.

> I have realised that I am the only owner of a design school, who is also a designer, globally, and the unique trait which is the core and strength of our business is that we believe in design, and we believe in good design. We live for design, design is the life cycle. I think the school would disappear in seconds if it didn't have designers at its absolute core.

Leanne is highly motivated by the industry in which she works and by her students. Her aspirations are to continue to expand the business and to continue training students to their full potential in design with a view to helping them to enjoy a lifetime in design.

> I think the most important thing is having seen so many fantastic students who usually start with very little creative confidence and at the end of three years, there's this incredible pride in being at the peak of their creative life and then watching them grow and run great businesses and work with great designers around the world. That's the most rewarding of all.

## 9.4 Leanne Whitehouse: The Entrepreneur

Leanne Whitehouse is a self-confident, energetic high achiever. She has a wealth of knowledge of the design and fashion industry, and in today's competitive environment, she has a keen sense of where the industry is going. She embraces innovation, change and adaptability, understands that the industry and education are in constant flux and aims for personal and professional growth and the sustainability of her educational venture (Fig. 9.3).

**Fig. 9.3** Leanne Whitehouse with acclaimed Italian fashion designer Rosita Missoni (Photo courtesy of Whitehouse Institute)

Leanne has always been passionate about fashion design and she has strived to make her ideas and dreams come true.

> I knew at four or five years of age I wanted to be a designer and I knew exactly what I wanted to do.

Driven by economic necessity to make a change in her life, equipped with a strong need to achieve on her own, Leanne relied on her valuable teaching and designing expertise and lengthy experience in the fashion industry, as well as her personal initiative, courage and self-confidence, to undertake the challenge of starting her own educational business.

> I am very self-confident, very driven and very competitive. I knew the students were there, I knew there was a need, I knew the market was there, and I wanted to get a business up and running because I had a new baby and was determined I'd do that by myself.

Although totally unprepared for the business side of the venture, she proved to be adaptable and learnt quickly on the job.

> I didn't know anything about business. It's been a tidal wave of learning. I think if I'd known how enormous commercial law, and accounting and all the things one needs to know in business I would've thought that's a mountain a little high for me to climb—but you just have to do it!

Leanne has a positive attitude to work and life. Highly focused and ambitious, she enjoys challenges, is open to innovation and is not intimidated by difficult situations.

I actually can't recall ever doubting. I never thought about looking back, I never thought about closing, or changing or pulling out, it's always just been 'let's go forward' and 'what's the next adventure?'.

Leanne is a natural leader, a doer, a visionary, but she is also aware that having a talented and supportive team of people alongside is crucial.

One of the great things, of course, is having great people that you work with. A common catch cry is 'oh, I love the business but not the people'. I don't say that of course, although managing people can be tricky, but that's something you learn. It's experience that gets you through.

Reflecting on the success of Whitehouse Institute, she believes that this is due fundamentally to her passion and vision for fashion design and her desire to impart her knowledge to young people who also love fashion and design.

If the teachers and staff don't love design it would be the wrong place for them to work. That love is very important.

She enjoys and admires the vitality, enthusiasm and initiative of young students and young designers.

There are so many talented, entrepreneurial, far-thinking young people who challenge your every thought; these kids are amazing.

Her goals and aspirations are to continue to grow and expand the Whitehouse Institute and to continue training students to their full potential in design with a view to helping them to enjoy a lifetime in design.

Leanne also recognises that she is intensely competitive and that her success is largely due to her motivation to excel.

I believe in always doing your best and trying to move forward. I'm not the person today I was 26 years ago, I'm a tougher, more driven and harder person. And determination is very important and keeping an open mind and being open to new experiences. So I think that determination and belief in design have been fundamental to the success of Whitehouse.

## 9.5 Recognition of Her Achievements

Leanne Whitehouse has had an extraordinary career, and her recognition for over 40 years of service as a designer, educator and business woman is well deserved (Fig. 9.4) (Frank, 2013).

In 2011, in recognition of her services to design education in Australia, Leanne was awarded the *Lifetime Achievement Award* by the Australian fashion industry

**Fig. 9.4** Leanne Whitehouse receives the *Lifetime Achievement Award* from Fashion Group International in 2011 (Photo courtesy of Whitehouse Institute)

## 9.5 Recognition of Her Achievements

**Fig. 9.5** Family portrait. Leanne Whitehouse with daughter Billie Whitehouse and poodle Lulu (Photo courtesy of Whitehouse Institute)

from the Fashion Group International[1] (Fig. 9.5) (ACPET, 2011). In accepting her award, she said that she was particularly pleased that the provision of quality education had been acknowledged by the fashion industry and that she was proud of the achievements of Australian graduate designers now working in Australia and internationally.

In 2014, Leanne became a member of the Australian Fashion Chamber (AFC) Board of Directors.

Reflecting on her achievements, Leanne does not like to dwell on it for long. She prefers to focus on future opportunities.

> I consider myself to be extremely fortunate that I've been able to do what I love doing every day, having the joy of learning and the joy of growing. And when some people say to me,

---

[1]The Fashion Group International (FGI) is a global professional organisation founded in 1930 in New York by a group of the most powerful fashion leaders in America including Elizabeth Arden, Helena Rubinstein and Eleanor Roosevelt to promote and benefit the fashion and design industry. FGI has over 5000 members in over 35 countries and continues to provide exciting professional and personal opportunities for career 'fashionistas' worldwide.

'Do you ever look at what you have created and how great it is?', I respond 'No, there is always too much to do. Always another goal to kick!'.

## References

ACPET. (2011, March 28). *Educator wins fashion award—Congratulations to Leanne Whitehouse*. ACPET. Accessed February 11, 2019, from http://www.acpet.edu.au/article/2379/educator-wins-fashion-award-congratulations-to-leanne-whitehouse/#sthash.XelrRaQW.dpuf

Casamento, J. (2012, June 17). At home with Leanne Whitehouse. *The Sydney Morning Herald*. Accessed February 21, 2019, from http://www.smh.com.au/lifestyle/fashion/at-home-with-leanne-whitehouse-20120616-20gik.htm

Frank, J. (2013, November 19). Leanne Whitehouse on 25 years of fostering Australian fashion. *Vogue*. Accessed February 21, 2019, from http://www.vogue.com.au/celebrity/interviews/leanne+whitehouse+on+25+years+of+fostering+australian+fashion,28303

Whitehouse Institute of Design, Australia. (n.d.). Accessed February 12, 2019, from https://whitehouse-design.edu.au/

# Conclusion 10

This book has provided an overview of the changing landscape of Australian tertiary education over the past 20 years. It has highlighted the important role that entrepreneurs have played in creating new educational businesses that have contributed to innovating and diversifying a sector which is facing new pressures and growing competition, by providing sustainable alternatives to traditional offerings. Due to changing patterns of student participation and expectations, shifts in student demographics and rapid technological changes, there is undeniably a demand for choice courses offered by independent institutions, and such alternatives have been well received by students who demand choice.

> Over recent years, independent education and training in Australia has been taken more seriously. Gradually there has been a growing awareness and recognition of its importance. That's been enormously encouraging for all of us, because apart from building a positive and reputable education option, you've got to survive as a business and you're only successful in education if you're successful in terms of business, you've got to be sustainable (Kay Ganley, Charlton Brown).

> We are certainly redefining our view of what the higher education sector is about (Mathew Jacobson, Ducere Global Business School).

> Education needs to be redefined at the moment. There are so many interesting things out there, some terrific opportunities to look at in terms of new educational models (Ryan Trainor, B-School).

The case studies selected for this book demonstrate a range of successful alternative educational options available to students in Australian tertiary education. Operating in an environment of growing globalisation and flexibility, the entrepreneurs in this book have worked creatively across strict limitations imposed by government and educational policy, as well as a strong regulatory framework, astutely recognising inefficiencies in the current tertiary education sector, identifying gaps and exploiting educational opportunities of untapped demand.

Relentlessly pursuing these new openings, they have introduced new products and services and created diverse for-profit educational models focused on tertiary student needs, which can offer more targeted education in areas of specialised study (e.g. music, digital media, natural therapies, photography, design, public safety, counselling and psychotherapy, theology), or areas more closely linked to employment, which have expanded the career prospects of many Australian and international students studying in Australia.

> We've opened up opportunities for many people. There are people who have had poor experiences in traditional education sectors, or people who are looking for something different, something more flexible, specific to their needs. That's what independent providers offer. There has been growing awareness of the importance of independent tertiary education in Australia, and the recognition that for most of us in this sector has been enormously encouraging (Kay Ganley, Charlton Brown).

> When I see an opportunity, a gap in the market, something that hasn't been done before in a certain way, I put a model together. It's really about coming up with the entrepreneurial idea and vision for a business that can be very successful (Mathew Jacobson, Ducere Global Business School).

Entrepreneurship literature acknowledges that business ideas are only the starting point and that it takes considerable effort to develop and fully implement the idea into a practical business (Carter, Gartner, & Reynolds, 1996; Gartner, 1985). These entrepreneurs have, over the years, invested large amounts of personal money, time and work into their ventures.

> We were really interested in job outcomes...We saw the opportunity. Philip, my brother, with his knowledge and background, and I sat down and crunched the numbers, over and over again, and did the risk analyses. The market was trending up, and we thought we could do it well (Mel Koumides, Academia 21).

> I knew nothing about business, absolutely nothing. I didn't have any furniture, so I went to an auction and bought all the furniture for the school. That was in 1988.... It took seven years of work for seven days a week for me. I would never consider taking a day off.... We went from being one little room in Liverpool Street in the city (of Sydney), to taking over most of the building, and having outgrown that building, we moved to our beautiful premises in Surrey Hills in Sydney (Leanne Whitehouse, Whitehouse Institute).

Entrepreneurs working in the tertiary independent education space have strong work ethic, have long working hours and have made sacrifices and experienced big challenges. Passion drives each one of them, and ambition to achieve their goals, regardless of the difficulties. As founders, they are the leaders and drivers of their venture and feel accountable and responsible as they have the highest stakes in their endeavour. Notwithstanding the failures they may have had, they are resilient and resourceful and have a strong determination and the drive to succeed.

# 10 Conclusion

> Success is the only way because failure never ever entered my head (Clive Langley, XLT).

> Actually I can't ever recall doubting. I never thought about looking back, I never thought about closing, or changing or pulling out, it's always just been 'let's go forward' and 'what's the next adventure? (Leanne Whitehouse, Whitehouse Institute).

Having created successful and sustainable businesses, these entrepreneurs cannot rest. They must stay ahead of the game. Working in a highly regulated environment, where change and tougher competition are inevitable, they need to remain agile, constantly transforming themselves and develop, redevelop and innovate in order to remain competitive and profitable.

> If we sit back and wait, suddenly it'll overwhelm you. There's no question. You need to adapt. Over the past 20 years the Navitas concept has been the same but there has been a huge adaptation of the model. Is it still relevant? There's no question, for now. Our growth has been phenomenal (Rod Jones, Navitas).

> We've been flexible, prepared to change. We have grown from a small eight-week nanny course; now we offer certificates, diplomas, online courses, and pathways into university. We have expanded from childcare, to aged care, disability, youth work, and community services. And now we offer our programs internationally. We work with orphanages, homes for the elderly, school teachers, in developing countries, but also in some developed countries (Kay Ganley, Charlton Brown).

> With my engineering background, I started offering welding courses, then moved on to underwater welding. Gradually we've developed ourselves into a very unique position. We're the only training company anywhere in the world that can train in underwater welding, titanium, plastics and polyethylene, seals and aluminium. We do the full scope. There's no one, no other company anywhere to compare. We work with large companies, international companies, we bring in technology that's new overseas (Clive Langley, XLT).

Relying on their experience, skills, general business expertise and entrepreneurial ability to exploit new opportunities that may present, they continue to be driven by their creativeness and opportunity obsession, but their behaviour is more calculated and targeted.

> What drives me is the idea and the opportunity, and being excited about doing something creative and innovative. I'm very interested in that creative aspect, you're creating something new that's not really been done before.... It's about the innovation, the idea, the creativity. What excites me in this business is that we have developed a completely new innovative business model (Mathew Jacobson, Ducere Global Business School).

> I love challenge, so to me, the thing that drives me is the next challenge. I'm passionate in what I want to do and I can't sit still. I love challenges in the sense of making something better and I think that's one of the things that Navitas has really given me. It's the growth and it's also taking it in different directions (Rod Jones, Navitas).

This book is a tribute to the passion and energy that dwells within them and at the centre of their work, drives their actions and achievements and injects renewed strength to pursue their goals.

I have to be constantly excited and passionate about what I am doing. What we are doing with Ducere has probably never been done anywhere in the world before (Mathew Jacobson, Ducere Global Business School).

First and foremost it's the love of design. That love is very important. Determination is also very important, keeping an open mind and being open to new experiences (Leanne Whitehouse, Whitehouse Institute).

It was the passion for jazz music, and the determination to learn that motivated me. And now it's the rewarding feeling of seeing someone else learn and grow. It's fantastic! (Greg Quigley, Jazz Music Institute).

I'm certainly passionate about education, and our business. We're really passionate about what we do (Kay Ganley, Charlton Brown).

While this has been only a limited work, the case studies presented offer a better understanding of how the participants view their individual entrepreneurial skills, what drives them and how they perceive their success and failures.

This book therefore makes an important contribution to works on entrepreneurship generally, and to tertiary education in particular, by venturing into a new sector that has not been previously studied. It acknowledges entrepreneurial individuals who have pushed the existing boundaries set by the traditional public sector, working creatively across strict limits imposed by government and educational policy, as well as a strong regulatory framework, and have, notwithstanding, made a fundamental, valuable contribution to the fast-evolving Australian tertiary education sector, as well as the community, and the national economy. This book celebrates their entrepreneurial spirit, success and achievements.

## References

Carter, N. M., Gartner, W. B., & Reynolds, P. D. (1996). Exploring start-up event sequences. *Journal of Business Venturing, 11*(3), 151–166.

Gartner, W. B. (1985). A conceptual framework for describing the phenomenon of new venture creation. *Academy of Management Review, 10*(4), 696–706.

Printed in the United States
By Bookmasters